The Origins of the Second World War

The Origins of the Second World War

Third Edition

Richard Overy

PEARSON
Longman

Harlow, England • London • New York • Boston • San Francisco • Toronto
Sydney • Tokyo • Singapore • Hong Kong • Seoul • Taipei • New Delhi
Cape Town • Madrid • Mexico City • Amsterdam • Munich • Paris • Milan

PEARSON EDUCATION LIMITED

Edinburgh Gate
Harlow CM20 2JE
Tel: +44 (0)1279 623623
Fax: +44 (0)1279 431059
Website: www.pearsoned.co.uk

First published in Great Britain in 1987
Second edition 1998
Third edition 2008

© Pearson Education Limited 1987, 1998, 2008

The right of Richard Overy to be identified as author of this work has been asserted
by him in accordance with the Copyright, Designs and Patents Act 1988.

ISBN: 978-1-4058-2469-9

British Library Cataloguing-in-Publication Data
A catalogue record for this book is available from the British Library

Library of Congress Cataloging-in-Publication Data
Overy, R. J.
    The origins of the Second World War / R.J. Overy. – 3rd ed.
        p. cm.
    Includes bibliographical references and index.
    ISBN-13: 978-1-4058-2469-9
    1. World War, 1939–1945 – Causes.   2. Europe – Politics and government – 1918–1945.
I. Title.
    D741.O84 2008
    940.53'11—dc22

2008006011

10   9   8   7   6
12

Typeset in 10/13.5pt Berkeley Book by 35
Printed and bound in Malaysia (CTP-VVP)

Introduction to the Series

History is a narrative constructed by historians from traces left by the past. Historical enquiry is often driven by contemporary issues and, in consequence, historical narratives are constantly reconsidered, reconstructed and reshaped. The fact that different historians have different perspectives on issues means that there is also often controversy and no universally agreed version of past events. *Seminar Studies in History* was designed to bridge the gap between current research and debate, and the broad, popular general surveys that often date rapidly.

The volumes in the series are written by historians who are not only familiar with the latest research and current debates concerning their topic, but who have themselves contributed to our understanding of the subject. The books are intended to provide the reader with a clear introduction to a major topic in history. They provide both a narrative of events and a critical analysis of contemporary interpretations. They include the kinds of tools generally omitted from specialist monographs: a chronology of events, a glossary of terms and brief biographies of 'who's who'. They also include bibliographical essays in order to guide students to the literature on various aspects of the subject. Students and teachers alike will find that the selection of documents will stimulate discussion and offer insight into the raw materials used by historians in their attempt to understand the past.

Clive Emsley and Gordon Martel
Series Editors

Contents

Preface

This is now the third preface in the history of this Seminar Studies volume, each separated by a decade of further scholarly argument about the issues that surround the coming of the Second World War. In this sense the preface is a kind of report on how the subject has developed, decade on decade. The changes have been far less dramatic in the ten years since the second edition. This is partly because much of the new archival material coming out of the former communist bloc had already been incorporated into the western writing in the 1990s, but it owes something to changing historical fashions. Diplomatic and military history no longer attracts the attention it got when this volume was first written. Historical writing has moved on to embrace many areas of experience that touch on issues of war only at a tangent. Nonetheless there have been important shifts in emphasis. The role of Italy in the approach to war has been subject to greater re-evaluation than any other; there are still revelations about Soviet policy in the 1930s, but above all the first serious studies of Soviet military planning and preparations; the arguments about Chamberlain and appeasement have become more sophisticated, and in an age where world war seems remote and unthinkable a new generation may think more kindly of his profound conviction that war was beyond all human reason. The question that may well tease historians now is simply why, if the overwhelming majority of people and rulers did not want war, their collective efforts were unable to achieve that end. For anyone who marched in 2003 against the Anglo-American war in Iraq, this question will have a particular echo.

In broad terms, however, the approach to the subject has not changed. Historians, whether they are sympathetic or not to the choices made by Britain and France in the 1930s, are generally agreed that domestic constraints played some part in shaping those decisions. The consequences of economic crisis and imperial insecurity are now central parts of any explanation of the international crisis in the 1930s, and particularly for the attitude of western governments to the change in the balance of power brought about by a resurgent Germany and an expansionist Italy and Japan. I have maintained the same broad analytical framework adopted in the first edition, with its emphasis on an international order in crisis, rather that the familiar tour through one episode after another in the 1930s. War in 1939 was not in any sense pre-determined. It emerged as a result of a complex interplay of a great many factors, but other outcomes might have been possible. I have tried to open up some of these different perspectives and in doing so to avoid distorting through hindsight the realities of the international order.

As before, I should like to offer here a general acknowledgement of my debt to other historians whose work I have compressed and simplified here, perhaps beyond recognition. My thanks go out to many colleagues and students who over the years have argued out the issues discussed here, disagreeing as often as not. I would like to thank Geoffrey Roberts for his kind assistance in improving the history of Soviet foreign policy in these pages. Though Roger Lockyer is no longer the general editor of the series, I remain grateful for all his encouragement and helpful editorial advice when this book went through its first edition.

Richard Overy
February 2008

Acknowledgements

The publishers would like to thank the following for permission to reproduce copyright material:

Extracts from an Air Staff memorandum (AIR 14/225), a memorandum for the chiefs of staff (AIR 9/105, pp. 6–7, 41) and a letter to Admiral Lord Chatfield (FO 371/23073, ff203–208), The National Archives, Crown copyright material in the Public Record Office is reproduced by permission of the Controller of Her Majesty's Stationery Office.

Plates 1, 2 and 6: Time & Life Pictures/Getty Images; Plates 3 and 7: Mary Evans Picture Library; Plate 4: Elkin, Vasilii, 'Every Kolkhoz Member, Every Brigade, Every MPS Must Know the Plan of Bolshevik Sowing'. International Poster Gallery: www.internationalposter.com; Plate 5: SV-Bilderdienst; Plate 8: Coloured photograph in 'Our Air force' (page 14), Mary Evans Picture Library.

Whilst every effort has been made to trace the owners of copyright material, in a few cases this has proved to be problematic and so we take this opportunity to offer our apologies to any copyright holders whose rights we may have unwittingly infringed.

Chronology

1914

28 June   Archduke Franz Ferdinand assassinated.

28 July   Austria declares war on Serbia.

4 August   All major European states at war.

1917

2 March   Tsar Nicholas abdicates.

25 October   Bolshevik Party seizes power in Russia.

1918

11 November   Armistice ends Great War.

1919

28 June   Signature of the Versailles Treaty (Paris Treaty) with Germany.

1920

10 January   League of Nations Organization begins its operations.

1922

6 February   Washington Naval Treaty signed.

28 October   March on Rome, Mussolini becomes Prime Minister.

1923

9 November   Hitler stages failed coup in Munich.

15 November   German currency collapses, end of hyperinflation.

1925

1 December Locarno Treaty signed between Britain, France, Germany, Italy and Belgium.

1926

24 April German-Soviet Treaty of Berlin.

10 September Germany joins the League of Nations.

1928

29 August Kellogg-Briand Pact signed in Paris outlawing war.

1929

29 October Start of 'great crash' on US stock exchange.

1931

September Japanese Kwantuing army seizes Manchuria.

1932

2 February Disarmament Conference convenes at Geneva.

9 July End of Lausanne Conference on reparations.

July/August British Commonwealth Ottawa Conference.

1933

30 January Hitler appointed German Chancellor.

12 June World Economic Conference in London.

15 July Four-Power Pact signed in Rome.

16 October Germany withdraws from League and from the Disarmament Conference.

1934

17 September Soviet Union admitted to the League of Nations.

5 December Franco-Soviet Pact.

1935

16 March Hitler announces German rearmament.

11 April Italy, Britain and France agree common front at Stresa Conference.

18 June Anglo-German Naval Agreement.

1935

6 February	Government of India Act gives limited autonomy.
3 October	Italy invades Abyssinia (Ethiopia).

1936

13 March	German forces remilitarize the Rhineland provinces.
17 July	Start of Spanish Civil War following failed military coup.
18 October	German second Four-Year Plan launched.
25 November	Anti-Comintern Pact signed between Germany and Japan.

1937

26 April	German aircraft bomb Basque city of Guernica.
1 May	United States permanent Neutrality Act passed.
9 July	Start of Sino-Japanese War.
November	Defence Requirements Committee set up in London.
13 December	Japanese capture Chinese capital of Nanking.

1938

13 March	Germany concludes *Anschluss* with Austria.
15 September	Chamberlain flies to meet Hitler in Germany.
22 September	Second Chamberlain/Hitler meeting.
30 September	Sudeten German areas ceded to Germany at Munich Conference.
30 September	Anglo-German agreement.
6 December	Franco-German Declaration signed.

1939

6 February	Chamberlain pledges military support for France.
15 March	German forces occupy Bohemia and Moravia.
21 March	Lithuanian city of Memel ceded to Germany.
23 March	German-Romanian trade agreement.
30 March	Italy occupies Albania.
31 March	Chamberlain guarantees Polish sovereignty.
26 April	Britain reintroduces conscription.
22 May	Pact of Steel between Italy and Germany.
23 August	German-Soviet Non-Aggression Pact signed in Moscow.

25 August	Anglo-Polish Treaty signed.
1 September	German forces attack Poland.
3 September	Britain and France declare war on Germany.
17 September	Red Army invades eastern Poland.
28 September	German-Soviet Treaty of Friendship divides Poland between them.
6 October	Hitler proposes 'peace' in German parliament.
10 October	Baltic States come under Soviet 'protection'.
30 November	Start of Soviet-Finnish War.
14 December	Soviet Union expelled from League of Nations.

1940

10 May	Chamberlain resigns, Churchill Prime Minister.
10 May	German forces attack the Netherlands, Belgium and France.
10 June	Italy declares war on Britain and France.
17 June	French sue for an armistice.
27 September	Tripartite Pact signed between Germany, Italy and Japan.
28 October	Italian invasion of Greece.
18 December	Hitler signs directive 'Barbarossa' for war against the Soviet Union.

1941

6 April	Germany invades Yugoslavia.
22 June	Germany and its allies invade Soviet Union.
12 August	Atlantic Charter published.
7 December	Japanese aircraft attack Pearl Harbor, USA declares war.
10 December	Germany and Italy declare war on the United States.

Who's Who

Baldwin, Stanley (1867–1947): Conservative politician who first entered the cabinet as President of the Board of Trade in 1921. He became Chancellor of the Exchequer a year later and then Prime Minister, a post he held from 1922 to 1924 and again from 1924 to 1929. He joined Ramsay MacDonald's National Government in 1931 as Lord President of the Council and Deputy Prime Minister, and became Prime Minister again from 1935 to his retirement in 1937. He was famous in 1932 for his announcement in the House of Commons that 'the bomber will always get through'.

Beck, Josef (1894–1944): Polish soldier and politician who became Polish Foreign Minister in 1932. He was determined to resist all political demands from either Germany or the Soviet Union and preferred war in 1939 rather than make concessions.

Beneš, Edouard (1884–1948): Czech politician who was Foreign Minister from 1918 to 1935, then President, following the death of Thomas Masaryk. He left Czechoslovakia in 1939 following German occupation and returned again as President briefly between 1946 and 1948 before the complete communist takeover.

Birkenhead, Earl of (1872–1930): The Conservative politician and lawyer F.E. Smith, who became Lord Chancellor in 1919 when he was ennobled, and between 1924 and 1928 was Secretary of State for India.

Bonnet, Georges (1889–1973): French Radical-Socialist politician. He was Finance Minister from 1937 to 1938, then Foreign Minister in Daladier's cabinet, where he campaigned for a full policy of appeasement. He supported the Vichy regime in 1940, and left France in 1944 before the Allied D-Day invasion.

Cadogan, Alexander (1884–1968): Permanent Under-Secretary at the British Foreign Office from 1938 to 1945, and Britain's representative at the United Nations between 1946 and 1950.

Chamberlain, Neville (1873–1940): Conservative politician from a prominent Birmingham political family. He was a successful minister in the 1920s, Chancellor of the Exchequer in 1934 (when he oversaw the programme of British rearmament) and from May 1937 Prime Minister in succession to Baldwin. He is seen as the architect of the policy of 'appeasement', but declared war on Germany in September 1939. He resigned in May 1940 and died later in the year.

Chiang Kai-shek (1887–1965): Chinese army officer who rose to power in China in the 1920s and fought a long civil war against Chinese communists and native warlords. He led Chinese resistance to Japanese invasion in the 1930s and 1940s but was defeated by communist insurgents in 1949 and retired to the island of Taiwan, which he ruled until his death.

Churchill, Winston (1874–1965): English politician, soldier and writer. He held high office before 1914 as a Liberal minister, saw service on the Western Front in 1916, before becoming Minister of Munitions. In the 1920s he became a Conservative and served as Chancellor of the Exchequer from 1926 to 1929. In the 1930s he was on the political fringes until the coming of war in 1939 when he took over the Admiralty. In May 1940 he became Prime Minister, a post that he held until 1945, and again from 1951 to 1955.

Ciano, Count Galeazzo (1903–44): Mussolini's son-in-law who was appointed Italian Foreign Minister in 1936, replacing Mussolini. He was less sanguine than Mussolini about Italy's prospects in war with the west. After Italy's surrender to the Allies in September 1943 he was arrested by the German-backed fascist regime set up in northern Italy and shot in 1944.

Dahlerus, Birger (1891–1957): Swedish businessman and a friend of Hermann Göring who acted unsuccessfully as an intermediary between Germany and Britain in the days before the outbreak of the Second World War.

Daladier, Edouard (1884–1970): French Radical Party politician who became Prime Minister as well as Minister of War in 1938 after the fall of the Popular Front government. He left office in May 1940 and was imprisoned by the Germans when France was occupied.

Eden, Anthony (1897–1977): Conservative politician who became Minister for the League of Nations in 1934 and Foreign Secretary in 1935, resigned in 1938 and was reinstated by Churchill in 1940. He was Prime Minister from 1955 to 1957.

Gamelin, General Maurice (1872–1958): French general who became Chief-of-Staff in 1936 and oversaw the rearmament of France in the late 1930s. He was replaced in the middle of the Battle of France in 1940 by

Marshal Maxime Weygand. The Vichy regime put him on trial and he was later deported to Germany.

Goering, Marshal Hermann (1893–1946): A successful fighter-pilot in the First World War, he joined the National Socialist Party in 1922 and rose to be one its senior politicians. In 1932 he was President of the Reichstag and following Hitler's appointment as Chancellor became a minister and, in 1935, Commander-in-Chief of the German Air Force. He committed suicide at Nuremberg in 1946 after being condemned to death for war crimes.

Grandi, Dino (1895–1988): Italian Fascist politician who became Foreign Minister from 1929 to 1932 and then Ambassador to London between 1932 and 1939. Grandi played an important part in forcing Mussolini from office in the summer of 1943 but then fled to Spain to avoid a death sentence from the new fascist regime set up in northern Italy with German support.

Halifax, Lord Edward (1881–1959): Senior Conservative politician, he was Viceroy to India in 1926–31 and then became Foreign Secretary in 1938 following Eden's resignation. He favoured limited appeasement and was replaced as Foreign Secretary by Eden late in 1940. He was posted to Washington as British Ambassador from 1941 to 1946.

Hankey, Maurice (1877–1963): Long-serving Secretary to the Committee for Imperial Defence from 1912–1938 and British Cabinet Secretary from 1916 to 1938. He was appointed to Chamberlain's war cabinet in 1939, but excluded when Churchill became Prime Minister.

Henderson, Nevile (1882–1942): British diplomat who became Ambassador to Berlin in 1937. He was widely regarded as being a pro-German appeaser, a reputation that has recently been reassessed. He delivered the British ultimatum to the German government on 3 September 1939.

Hirohito, Emperor of Japan (1901–89): The last traditional emperor of Japan, he oversaw Japanese expansion in the 1930s and agreed to the war with the United States in 1941. In 1945 he announced Japanese surrender but was allowed to remain in office as a constitutional head of state.

Hitler, Adolf (1889–1945): Austrian-born politician who came to Germany in 1913, served in a Bavarian regiment during the First World War and joined the tiny German Workers' Party in 1919. The party became the National Socialist Party (NSDAP) two years later with Hitler at its head. He attempted a coup in 1923 and was imprisoned. He took control of the party again in 1926, and seven years later was appointed German Chancellor. He became dictator of Germany and embarked on a programme of rearmament, territorial expansion and anti-Semitism. He attacked Poland in 1939 and launched world war. In 1941 he initiated what became the Holocaust and in April 1945 committed suicide in the ruins of Berlin.

Hull, Cordell (1871–1955): American Democrat politician who became Roosevelt's Secretary of State from 1932 until 1944, when ill-health forced him to retire. He was committed to the belief that all conflicts have economic causes and that worldwide prosperity would bring peace. He was awarded the Nobel peace prize in 1945.

Inskip, Thomas (1876–1947): Conservative politician and lawyer who was appointed as Minister for the Co-ordination of Defence from 1936 to 1939, and then became Lord Chancellor from 1939 to 1941. His role in promoting British rearmament was widely condemned as too little, too late.

King, Mackenzie (1874–1950): Canadian Liberal politician who was Prime Minister three times, the third time from 1935 to 1948 when he played an important part in persuading Canadian opinion to follow Britain into war in 1939 and offering extensive financial and material aid during the war.

Krosigk, Schwerin von (1887–1977): German Finance Ministry official who was appointed Finance Minister in Germany in 1932 and kept the office until 1945. He was responsible for helping to finance German rearmament and the financial exploitation of Europe but avoided indictment as a major war criminal at Nuremberg in 1945.

Lenin (Vladimir Ulyanov) (1870–1924): Chairman of the Russian Social Democratic Party (Bolsheviks) and the most influential theoretical Marxist of his generation. He encouraged the party to launch the revolution in October 1917 and became the leader of the new government until illness in 1922 forced him to withdraw from active politics.

Litvinov, Maxim (1876–1951): Russian Bolshevik politician and diplomat. He was appointed Foreign Minister in 1930 but replaced in March 1939. He later served as Soviet Ambassador to the United States from 1941 to 1943.

Lyautey, Marshal Hubert (1854–1934): French general who spent most of his army career in the colonies. He became the first Resident-General in French Morocco from 1912 to 1925.

Molotov, Vyacheslav (1890–1986): Bolshevik politician and close associate of Stalin, whose secretariat he served in the 1920s. He was made Chairman of the Council of People's Commissars in 1930 (Prime Minister) until 1941, and was also Commissar for Foreign Affairs from 1939 until 1949.

Morgenthau, Henry (1891–1967): American Democrat politician who became Treasury Secretary in the Roosevelt government from 1934 to 1945.

He is best remembered for his 'plan' to turn Germany into an agrarian state after the war as a punishment.

Mussolini, Benito (1883–1945): Radical socialist politician from the Romagna province who became a nationalist in response to the First World War. He fought at the front and returned to found the Italian fascist movement in 1919. In October 1922 he was appointed Prime Minister, established a single-party dictatorship by 1926 and led Italy into wars in Ethiopia (1935), Spain (1936–9) and against the western powers (1940–3). He was overthrown by a military coup in 1943 and killed by Italian anti-fascist partisans in April 1945.

Pétain, Marshal Phillipe (1856–1951): French general who played an important part in the French war effort in the First World War. He oversaw the building of the Maginot defences, but retired from the army in the 1930s. In June 1940 he assumed the role of head-of-state with his capital in the French town of Vichy. In 1945 he was arrested and sentenced to life imprisonment for political crimes committed under his authoritarian rule.

Ribbentrop, Joachim von (1893–1946): A former champagne salesman who became a leading National Socialist spokesman on foreign affairs after 1933. He was appointed Ambassador to London in 1936, and in 1938 was appointed German Foreign Minister. Dominated by Hitler, he played little part in key decision making. He was tried at Nuremberg and sentenced to death.

Rommel, Field Marshal Erwin (1891–1944): German career soldier who rose to prominence as a tank commander in the early stages of the Second World War. He was posted to head German forces in North Africa in 1941, but was defeated by British Commonwealth forces at El Alamein. He was implicated in the July Plot to murder Hitler in 1944 and committed suicide.

Roosevelt, Franklin Delano (1882–1945): A prominent Democrat politician who served under Woodrow Wilson as Assistant Secretary for the Navy in the First World War. After struggling against polio in the 1920s, he became first Governor of New York State in 1928 and four years later was elected US President. He held the office for an unprecedented four terms, and played an important role in holding together the wartime Grand Alliance with Britain and the USSR.

Schacht, Hjalmar (1877–1970): German banker who was chosen to help solve the inflation crisis in Germany in late 1923, then to head the German Central Bank. He was appointed Minister of Economics in Hitler's government in 1934 and in 1935 Plenipotentiary for War Economy. He helped to supply the finance for German rearmament, but he fell out with Hitler in

1937 and resigned. He was later arrested and tried at Nuremberg but was one of three defendants acquitted.

Speer, Albert (1905–81): German architect who was commissioned by Hitler to help rebuild Germany's largest cities in the 1930s. He was appointed Armaments Minister in February 1942, and was later tried at Nuremberg, where he was sentenced to twenty years.

Stalin (Joseph Dzhugashvili) (1878–1953): Georgian Marxist who joined the Russian Social Democratic Party, followed Lenin when the party split over tactics in 1904 and became Commissar for Nationalities in the first Bolshevik government in November 1917. In 1922 he was appointed General Secretary of the party and used this position to help him to establish a personal dictatorship in the Soviet Union from the 1930s to the 1950s. He was Prime Minister from 1941 until his death in 1953, and Commissar for Defence from 1941 to 1946.

Taylor, Alan J.P. (1906–90): British historian who taught at Manchester and Oxford. He was famous for a controversial book on the outbreak of war published in 1961, which claimed that Hitler was no more to blame for the war than Britain and France.

Tojo, General Hideki (1884–1948): Japanese soldier and politician who became Minister of War in July 1940 and then Prime Minister in October 1941 shortly before the Japanese attack on Pearl Harbor. He resigned in July 1944, following Japanese defeats, and was tried and executed as a war criminal in 1948.

Trotsky, Leon (1879–1940): Russian socialist belonging to the Menshevik wing of the party. He became a Bolshevik in 1917 and commanded the Red Army during the Russian Civil War. He resigned in 1925 and was then accused of left-wing deviation, expelled from the party and sent into exile in 1929. He was assassinated in Mexico by a Stalinist agent in 1940.

Wilson, Woodrow (1856–1924): Democrat politician who became President of the United States from 1913 to 1921. He played a major part in shaping the postwar settlement in Europe with his insistence on 'self-determination', but the US Senate rejected the Versailles Settlement in 1920.

Glossary

Anglo-German Agreement: Paper signed by Hitler and Chamberlain in the early hours of of 30 September 1938 after the Munich Conference, renouncing war between the two states and agreeing to settle issues by negotiation. This was the 'scrap of paper' Chamberlain waved when he arrived back in England later that day.

Anschluss: Literally the 'joining on' of Austria to Germany after German troops occupied the country on 12 March 1938.

Appeasement: British and French attempts to satisfy or 'appease' the demands of aggressor nations during the 1930s.

Atlantic Charter: Declaration prepared by Churchill and Roosevelt at their meeting in Placentia Bay, Newfoundland, 9–12 August 1941. The Charter was a commitment to promoting the self-determination of peoples and democratic institutions.

Autarky: A policy of economic self-sufficiency, made at the expense of international trade.

Blitzkrieg: Literally 'lightning war', the term was commonly used in the early 1940s to describe the new form of fast, mobile warfare supported by aircraft which could bring a result in a matter of weeks. The model was the German invasion of Poland.

Collective security: The idea that international peace could be preserved by all states co-operating together to restrain an international aggressor. It was chiefly associated with the League of Nations.

Comintern: The Third International of communists, set up by Lenin in 1919 to succeed the defunct Second International. It became an instrument for Soviet control of other communist parties and was wound up in 1943.

Condor Legion: A unit of several thousand German airmen sent to Spain in 1936 to assist Franco's rebellion against the republican government.

Commanded by Werner von Richthofen, the Legion was notorious for the bombing of the Basque city of Guernica on 26 April 1937.

Congress System: The international order in Europe after the Napoleonic Wars when the Great Powers tried to solve issues through a series of congresses. The name was often applied to the whole of the nineteenth century to explain the long period of general European peace.

Co-Prosperity Sphere: Sphere of influence set up by Japan in Asia in the late 1930s. The idea was to demonstrate to other Asian states that they would all benefit from the Japanese domination of the region through building an integrated economic bloc, but the system was designed chiefly to benefit Japan.

Danzig: Ancient German city declared a 'free city' under the League of Nations in the Versailles Settlement in June 1919. By 1933 its parliament was dominated by local National Socialists who made life difficult for the Polish minority in the city and demanded union with Hitler's Germany.

Détente: Name given to the efforts to scale down the Cold War from the late 1960s, but applied to any diplomatic effort to reduce tension and reach accommodation.

Disarmament Conference: Conference convoked through the auspices of the League of Nations in February 1932 under the chairmanship of the Labour politician Arthur Henderson. It failed to reach agreement on any measure of arms reduction and adjourned in October 1933 without reconvening.

Four-Year Plan: Plan for economic and military preparation for war drawn up by Hitler in August 1936 and formally launched under the direction of Hermann Göring in October. It was strictly speaking the second Four-Year Plan, following the first Four-Year Plan launched in 1933 to overcome unemployment.

German inflation: The collapse of the German currency (the mark) in November 1923 following almost ten years of escalating inflation, chiefly caused by huge government borrowing during the war. The currency was stabilized in 1924 with international help, but a generation of German savers and investors was ruined.

German-Soviet Non-Aggression Pact: Agreement between Germany and the USSR signed on 23 August 1939 agreeing not to resort to war. The treaty also contained a trade agreement and a secret protocol dividing eastern Europe into spheres of influence. It was followed by a firm agreement on the new frontier in Poland signed on 28 September 1939.

Grand Settlement: Term used by Neville Chamberlain to describe a multilateral negotiated settlement of all outstanding issues of frontiers, minorities, access to markets and raw materials, replacing the Versailles Settlement of 1919.

'Have-not' nations: Major states that lacked a large territorial empire or adequate access to raw materials or markets. These contrasted with the 'have' states of Britain, France and the United States.

Imperial Preference: Protective trade system agreed by Britain and the Dominions at the Ottawa Imperial Conference in 1932. Britain agreed to give preference to imperial imports of food and raw materials and the Dominions agreed to take more British industrial goods.

Isolationism: The popular American view in the 1920s and 1930s that the United States should avoid any foreign political or military commitments.

July Crisis: The month-long diplomatic crisis following the assassination of the Habsburg Archduke Franz Ferdinand on 28 June 1914 in Sarajevo. The crisis paved the way for the outbreak of the First World War.

Lebensraum: Term commonly used in Germany in the 1920s and 1930s to describe that amount of territory thought to be necessary to allow a nation to feed and provision itself to a reasonable standard. The search for 'living space' became the excuse for programmes of territorial expansion. In Italy the concept was called il spazio vitale.

Maginot Line: A series of defensive fortifications along France's eastern border, begun at the inspiration of the Defence Minister, André Maginot, in 1929, but still incomplete a decade later.

Mandates: Colonies and territories taken under League control from Germany and Turkey in 1919. They were allocated as 'mandates' to Britain, France and Japan, who were responsible for their administration though they were not formally part of their empires. In practice they were treated like colonial territories except for Iraq, which was granted its full independence in 1932.

Mitteleuropa: The area of central Europe including Germany, Austria, Hungary and Poland. It was usually regarded as a potential economic bloc and a sphere for German influence, rather than an area of political influence implied by the term Lebensraum.

Munich Agreement: Protocol signed by Germany, Britain, France and Italy on the evening of 29 September 1938 granting self-determination under German control to the German inhabitants of the Czech state, most of them in the area known as the Sudetenland.

New Deal: Package of economic and welfare policies instituted by President Roosevelt in 1933–4 following his election, to try to cope with the social consequences of the slump.

New Order: Term usually associated with fascist plans for a new social order or a new international order. The 'old' order was in both cases identified with the political system of the west and its traditional European empires.

Non-Intervention: Agreement reached between all the major states in late 1936 not to intervene militarily in the Spanish Civil War. Only Britain and France observed the agreement. Italy, Germany and the Soviet Union all gave aid to one side or the other.

Open-door policy: A system in which all states can trade on the basis of the same 'open' access to another market. The term is usually used to describe efforts to trade on equal terms with China.

Operation Barbarossa: Code name given to the German invasion of the USSR. The directive for the operation was laid down by Hitler on 18 December 1940, and the invasion by 4 million German, Hungarian, Romanian and Finnish forces began on 22 June 1941.

Pan-Germanism: The concept of uniting all ethnic Germans in a single political unit. There were Pan-German movements in pre-1914 Germany and Austria which influenced Hitler's later Pan-German aspirations in the 1930s.

Phoney War: The period between September 1939 and May 1940 when there was very little military activity between Germany, Britain and France.

Polish Corridor: Narrow strip of land carved out of the former German province of East Prussia to allow the newly formed Polish state access to the sea. The corridor divided eastern and western parts of Germany and became a key issue on treaty revision in the 1930s.

Polish Guarantee: Name given to the announcement by Neville Chamberlain in the House of Commons on 31 March 1939 that Poland's sovereignty would be guaranteed by Britain. France pledged similar support a few days later, but a firm Anglo-Polish Treaty was only signed on 25 August, a few days before the German invasion.

Popular Front: Term used in 1935 to describe the political alliance between progressive political forces, principally social-democrats and communists, to combat the threat of fascism. It is usually applied to the French government elected in 1935 and the Spanish government elected in 1936.

Reparations: Payments in kind and money demanded by the victorious Allies in 1919 from Germany and its allies. Reparations were paid by Bulgaria, Hungary, and Austria, but the bulk were extracted from Germany, who continued to pay them until 1932 when economic crisis forced a moratorium.

Sanctions: The policy of imposing an economic and financial boycott against states engaged in aggressive war in violation of the Covenant of the League of Nations. It was applied only to Italy during the Italo-Ethiopian War.

Schlieffen Plan: Not so much a plan, as a set of operational suggestions first proposed by the German army Chief-of-Staff, Alfred von Schlieffen in 1904 as an answer to German encirclement by France and Russia. The plan was based on the idea of a swift defeat of France, followed by a redeployment to face and defeat Russia. It failed in 1914, turning the war into a contest of attrition.

Soviet purges: Term loosely used to describe the period 1936–8 when almost 700,000 were executed by the Soviet judicial system for alleged crimes against the state. The victims included many Communist Party leaders and a high proportion of the leadership of the army and navy.

Spanish Civil War: Conflict between rebel nationalist forces led by General Franco and the armed forces and irregular socialist and anarchist militia in support of the Spanish Second Republic. The nationalist revolt began in July 1936 and ended with Franco's victory in March 1939.

Sudeten Germans: German-speaking population of northern Bohemia who were placed under Czechoslovak rule in 1919 when the Habsburg Empire was formally partitioned in the Versailles Settlement.

Thirty-Years' War: European-wide conflict in Europe between 1618 and 1648 which was characterized by extreme levels of violence against the civilian population.

Total War: Term usually associated with the German general Erich Ludendorff, who in 1919 described the First World War as a 'total war' because it had demanded the total commitment of the economic, social and moral resources of the nation. It also described a war in which civilians as well as soldiers were part of the war effort and a legitimate target of attack.

Tripartite Pact: Agreement signed between Germany, Italy and Japan on 27 September 1940 dividing the world into spheres of influence between them. Hungary, Romania and Slovakia later affiliated to the Pact.

Versailles Settlement: Set of treaties drawn up by the Allied powers in 1919 at the Versailles palace, outside Paris. The treaties included the Paris Treaty with Germany, the St Germain Treaty with Austria and the Treaty of Trianon with Hungary.

Washington Conference: Multinational conference on the limitation of naval armaments held in Washington in November 1921 and signed in early 1922. The conference set down the ratio of warships between Britain, Japan, the United States and France.

Wehrwirtschaft: Term used to describe an economy geared to defence purposes, with a high level of investment, heavy industrial output and extensive plans for the conversion of civilian to military production in the event of war.

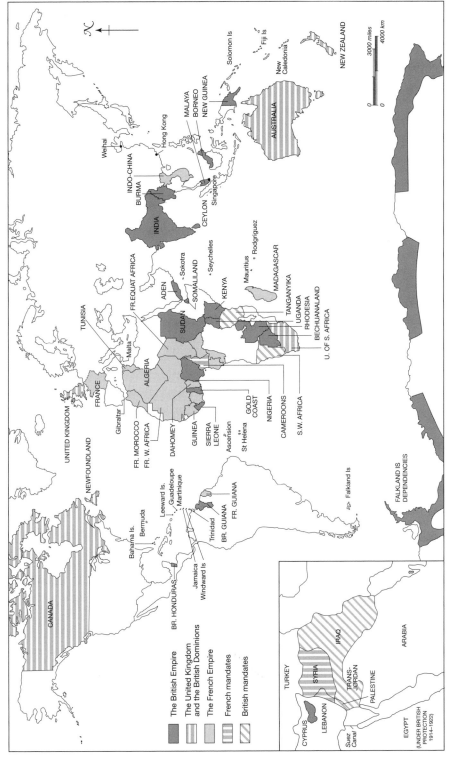

Map 1 The British and French Empires between the two world wars

Map 2 The Japanese Empire by 1941

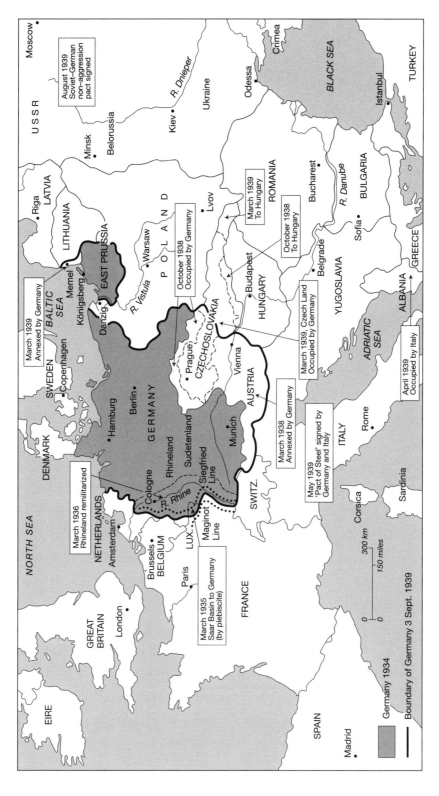

Map 3   Germany and Central Europe 1933–39

Part 1

BACKGROUND

1

Explaining the Second World War

The Second World War once seemed a simple event to explain. If it did not exactly boil down to one word – **Hitler** – the war was nevertheless the Germans' war. Unlike the war of 1914, that of 1939 had a simple reducible core: Germany provoked war deliberately to overturn the **Versailles Settlement** of 1919 and win the continental hegemony denied it in 1914. Moreover, the Germany of 1939 was led by a party committed, so it seemed, to a demonstrably evil cause. Fighting Germany, and later Italy and Japan, was to fight on the side of good in the defence of democracy and freedom, against what **President Roosevelt** called 'the forces endeavouring to enslave the entire world' (Roosevelt, 1938–50: vol. 8, 639).

For all its simplicity there is much to recommend this view. Without Hitler's restless quest for empire, war might have been avoided. If the western powers had not been faced with an accumulation of crisis after crisis in central Europe, which built up almost irresistible pressure for conflict by 1939, German aims might have been accommodated in the international system without war. This is, of course, a very large 'if'. In practice the outbreak of war was a great deal more complicated than this. Historians cannot even agree on the nature of the pressures that pushed Hitler towards war. While some see a clear intention on his part to launch wars of aggression, based on the ideas of racial struggle and world empire expressed in Hitler's writing and speeches, others emphasize the importance of functional explanations, that German leaders were forced into war in 1939 through fear of domestic unrest and economic crisis brought about by the excessive cost of rearmament. Nor can agreement be reached on the kind of war Hitler launched: was it a total war which required the full use of the nation's resources to fight the great powers for world status? Or a *Blitzkrieg*, a short opportunistic war, designed to avert domestic political pressure by using a minimum of military resources for the campaign?

Arguments such as these mask a more important problem in explaining the outbreak of war. By concentrating on Germany we are in danger of

Hitler, Adolf (1889–1945): Austrian-born politician who became leader of the National Socialist Party (NSDAP) in 1922. In 1933 he was appointed German Chancellor and became dictator of Germany. He attacked Poland in 1939 and launched world war. In 1941 he initiated what became the Holocaust and in April 1945 committed suicide in the ruins of Berlin.

Versailles Settlement: Set of treaties drawn up by the Allied powers in 1919 at the Versailles palace, outside Paris. The treaties included the Paris Treaty with Germany, the St Germain Treaty with Austria and the Treaty of Trianon with Hungary.

Roosevelt, Franklin Delano (1882–1945): Prominent Democrat politician who became first Governor of New York State in 1928 and four years later was elected US President. He held the office for an unprecedented four terms, and played an important role in holding together the wartime Grand Alliance with Britain and the USSR.

Blitzkrieg: Literally 'light-ning war', the term was commonly used in the early 1940s to describe the new form of fast, mobile warfare supported by aircraft which could bring a result in a matter of weeks. The model was the German invasion of Poland.

Collective security: The idea that international peace could be preserved by all states co-operating together to restrain an international aggressor. It was chiefly associ-ated with the League of Nations.

Chamberlain, Neville (1873–1940): Conservat-ive politician who became Chancellor of the Ex-chequer in 1934 (when he oversaw the programme of British rearmament) and from May 1937 Prime Minister in succession to Baldwin. He is seen as the architect of the policy of 'appeasement', but declared war on Germany in September 1939.

Taylor, Alan J.P. (1906–90): British historian who taught at Manchester and Oxford. He was famous for a controversial book on the outbreak of war published in 1961, which claimed that Hitler was no more to blame for the war than Britain and France.

forgetting that wars do not take place in a vacuum. Germany was part, and quite a small part, of an international system. German statesmen reacted to problems and stimuli over which, in many cases, they had no control. Hitler planned to subvert a structure of world power for which Germany had very little responsibility except that it had lost, rather than won, the First World War. To understand the outbreak of war in Europe in 1939, and its extension within two years to world war, it is necessary to look at the international structure as a whole, its weaknesses and strengths, and at the character and motives of the major powers that comprised it.

It must not be forgotten that war in 1939 was declared by Britain and France on Germany, and not the other way round. A large part of any explanation for the war that broke out in September 1939 must rest on this central point. Why did the two western powers go to war with Germany? Immediately the question is put this way round, the role of Germany assumes a new and very different perspective. France and Britain had com-plex interests and motives for war. They, too, had to take decisions on inter-national questions with one eye on public opinion and domestic politics and another on potential enemies elsewhere. The traditional picture of the western democracies acting as honest brokers in world affairs, vainly trying to uphold the spirit of the Covenant of the League of Nations and the strat-egy of '**collective security**' in the face of totalitarian pressure can no longer be upheld. Nor can the later view that saw **Chamberlain** and his cabinet as 'Guilty Men', honest but incompetent appeasers, willing to give the dictators what they wanted until forced by the moral indignation of popular opinion to fight. Instead historians now emphasize that French and British foreign policy in the 1930s was the product of a complex interplay of domestic and international pressures and interests which cannot be adequately sub-sumed in the popular notion of appeasement. It was in fact, as **A.J.P. Taylor** pointed out to public dismay in 1961, old-fashiond balance-of-power politics (Taylor, 1961).

The significance of Taylor's argument was that it forced people to see that British and French policy before 1939 was governed primarily by *raisons d'état*, and only secondarily by moral considerations. In other words the British and the French, just like the Germans, were anxious to preserve or extend their power, and safe-guard their economic interests, by a variety of means, some much less scrupulous than others. If, in the end, this meant going to war to preserve Franco-British power and prestige, it also meant finding ways of containing or accommodating other powers in a system still dominated by British and French interests. If Chamberlain has not been com-pletely exonerated by recent historiography, appeasement now seems a far less reprehensible strategy than it did a generation ago. Indeed it can now be seen to be very much in the mainstream of the British diplomatic tradition.

When the explanation for the outbreak of war moves beyond Germany to Britain and France, it at once assumes a global significance. Both the western powers were possessors of empires that stretched across the world. They faced problems not just in central Europe but in the Near East, the Middle East and throughout Africa. The interests of these areas had to be balanced against those nearer home. In the Far East the imperial powers came directly into contact with the two major Pacific powers, Japan and the United States, who both had divergent interests of their own. In Asia and the Middle East Britain and France looked warily towards the Soviet Union and the unpredictable effects of international communism. In areas remote from Europe the German threat was peripheral, to say the least. British diplomacy was based on a global strategy of which the German question formed a part, and until 1935 a subordinate part. If France was more immediately concerned with German revisionism, it was also a major imperial power threatened by the rise of **Mussolini**'s Italy in the Mediterranean and by the insecurity of its African and Asian empire. It was the global character of these responsibilities which eventually turned a conflict in Europe over German power into a world war.

Holding all the powers loosely together was the international economy. With the growth of world trade and investment, economic questions impinged on diplomacy in a very direct way. The distribution of the economic spoils, the rise and fall of the international business cycle, deeply affected political decisions and involved all the powers, willy-nilly, in a constant round of economic argument. The powers were compelled to bind their diplomatic and economic interests more closely together. Much of the recent history on the outbreak of war has exposed the importance of 'economic diplomacy', or 'economic appeasement'. There is no doubt that economic rivalry and economic dependence played a major part in the international crisis of the 1930s, adding a new dimension to conflicts which have hitherto been regarded more as the product of military and territorial ambition, or the defence of status and prestige.

There are strong echoes here of the crisis that resulted in war in 1914. That is not to say that the war of 1914–18 or the postwar settlement at Versailles in any direct sense *caused* the outbreak of the Second World War. But both global conflicts were the product of an age of rapid political, economic and diplomatic change which provided the context within which specific crises had to be confronted. Both wars to be fully understood have to be set against this background.

In the years before 1914 the international system was faced with growing crisis. For most of the nineteenth century the major European powers, loosely orchestrated first by Metternich, then by Bismarck, had worked together in concert, designed to maintain the existing distribution of influence among

Mussolini, Benito (1883–1945): Radical socialist politician who founded the Italian fascist movement in 1919. In 1922 he was appointed Prime Minister, established a single-party dictatorship by 1926 and led Italy into wars in Ethiopia (1935), Spain (1936–9) and against the western powers (1940–3). He was overthrown by a military coup in 1943 and killed by partisans in April 1945.

the traditional great powers, and to prevent a return to the warfare and political uncertainty of the French revolutionary years. Though there were plenty of minor disagreements, there was a broad consensus among the ruling class groups who dominated foreign policy about the need to maintain a balance of power. With the rise of Germany and the United States, the modernization of Tsarist Russia and Japan and Europe's rapid industrialization, the equilibrium was undermined. In the search for greater security and economic advantage the European powers looked to imperialism. Some, like Britain and France, had old-established empires and could build upon them, hesitantly and often incoherently, in order to enhance their power. Other states rapidly followed, deeming empire to be the explanation for British economic strength and international preponderance. By the 1890s the concert had been replaced by intense diplomatic and economic rivalry, and the growth of a system of fixed alliances. Though the powers still could, and did, co-operate to solve international crises, they resorted increasingly to secret diplomacy, exclusive treaties and, in the end, to an arms race (Langhorne, 1981).

None of this made the outbreak of war inevitable, but it made it much more likely. So, too, did the sharp changes in domestic politics. By the 1890s the tide of democracy and nationalism could no longer be ignored. The traditional ruling houses of Europe found themselves faced with the prospect of the imminent collapse of the old political structure through pressure from middle-class democrats and nationalists and the new working class thrown up by economic growth. International crisis thus assumed a new dimension. War, or the prospect of war, might destroy the old regimes altogether, or might, it was argued, give them a renewed lease of life. Faced with such a choice the Habsburgs, under mounting pressure from nationalists within the Empire and without, opted for war in July 1914 rather than accept the final erosion of Habsburg power. For once, feeble efforts at concerted action by the other powers broke down. The Serbian crisis interlocked with the wider system of rivalries and alliances, and could then not be reversed. By August 1914 all the great powers were at war for the first time since 1815.

At the end of the war Allied statesmen hoped to be able to turn the clock back to the nineteenth-century equilibrium, to a world widely regarded as the model of 'progress and harmony' (Thomson, 1960). The defeat of the most threatening of the new powers, Germany, contributed to the sense that the old concert could be resurrected, operated by Britain and France together with other peace-loving nations. The peace settlement drawn up at Versailles in the spring of 1919 reflected the Allies' ambition to prevent Germany ever threatening peace again [**Doc. 1, p. 102**]. The German signatories to the treaty were compelled to admit German responsibility for the war and had to accept the country's economic and military enfeeblement, and extensive territorial losses. The treaty also provided for the establishment of a League of

Nations under whose auspices the peace could be kept by the collective action of all those states willing to subscribe to a future of peaceful collaboration. Like Metternich's '**Congress System**' in the early nineteenth century, the League system relied on the goodwill and self-restraint of the world's major powers.

The commitment to security and peaceableness was strengthened by two further agreements. In early 1922, following a conference in **Washington**, treaty arrangements were made for the future security of the Pacific region and eastern Asia. In 1925 the European great powers agreed in the Treaty of Locarno to guarantee the frontiers of western Europe against aggression, which opened the way to further *rapprochement* between the former enemies of 1918. In Paris four years later sixty-five nations, including Germany, Japan and the Soviet Union, signed the Kellog-Briand Pact condemning the use of war as an instrument of state policy. There existed widespread popular support for peaceful collaboration. In Britain the League of Nations Union reached a peak of 400,000 members in 1933. The No More War Movement and the War Resisters' International both advocated more radical forms of non-compliance, including refusal to serve in the armed forces. In France more than a million marched through Paris in the summer of 1936 in support of international peace. Pacifist movements in Europe and America applauded the new spirit of reconciliation and internationalism and benefited from the widespread revulsion against the prospect of another major war. They were weakened only by the difficulty of reconciling absolute pacifists, who opposed any use of violence, with those pacifists who believed that an international police force of some kind (empowered to coerce if it had to) would be the best way to isolate and punish the aggressor. During the 1930s pacifists spent as much time fighting each other as they did confronting the threat of war.

The statesmen who dominated the international system in the 1920s shared a common set of assumptions which could be traced directly back to the world of imperialism and economic rivalry in which they had been brought up before 1914. The year 1918 had been a dividing line of sorts, but not a decisive one. In many cases diplomacy was still dominated by the small specialized élites which ran the foreign offices and diplomatic corps before the war. They all shared the view that the international system was dominated by a small group of great powers, and that the desirable course was to establish, by agreement if possible, some sort of balance between them. Though many politicians shared the revulsion against war, a willingness to resort to force *in extremis* was an essential part of the balance and conformed with the still powerful role of the military in European public life. Most European statesmen subscribed, to greater or lesser degree, to a sense of racial and cultural superiority. In the interwar years there was nothing exclusively German

Congress System: The international order in Europe after the Napoleonic Wars when the Great Powers tried to solve issues through a series of congresses. The name was often applied to the whole of the nineteenth century to explain the long period of general European peace.

Washington Conference: Multinational conference on the limitation of naval armaments held in Washington in November 1921 and signed in early 1922. The conference set down the ratio of warships between Britain, Japan, the United States and France.

about this. It was widely assumed that European culture was more enlightened and progressive than that of other races despite the evident moral crisis provoked by the horrors of the recent war. Outside Europe white rule was held to be in the interest of everybody, ruler and subject alike. Imperialism had its practical side as well. It provided an outlet for emigration and trade from Europe, and gave guaranteed access to markets and raw materials. Although many of the assumptions about empire proved illusory, this crude geo-political view was deeply rooted in the European mind. The physical possession of territory was still considered a vital interest, a source of prestige and a key to economic growth. In 1937 Neville Chamberlain, the British Prime Minister, argued that in a united empire 'lies the seat of our influence in the world' (Tamchina, 1972: 100).

Just as the values of the prewar world survived into the 1920s, so too did its problems. In practice the equilibrium of the postwar period masked the continuing fragility of the international system. The war had brought about dramatic changes but had solved little. The old dynastic states of central and eastern Europe had disappeared – the Habsburg Empire, the Russian Empire, Imperial Germany – but the problems of nationalist rivalry in the region and the future of German and Russian power had been postponed rather than resolved. Although Britain and France were the direct beneficiaries of the war, the problems of being the major imperial powers had multiplied. Both empires reached their fullest extent in the 1920s with the acquisition of German colonies and the break up of what had been left of the Turkish Empire. But both empires were now under attack by those same forces, nationalism and political liberalism, which had previously undermined the stability of pre-1914 Europe. In the Middle East, which both Britain and France viewed as vital to the preservation of their global influence, long-standing conflicts in Palestine, Egypt and Syria were now joined with new demands for political independence. Both the European powers were committed to empires whose security and integrity it was difficult to defend. Only the weakness of the defeated powers, and Russia's temporary eclipse, disguised this fact.

For much of the 1920s international affairs were conducted in a vacuum. Britain and France achieved a predominance quite out of proportion to their real strengths because of the temporary unwillingness or inability of the other powers to intervene decisively in world politics. The great-power system was played with only two of the major states committed fully to maintaining it. The position of the Soviet Union illustrates this. In the aftermath of the Bolshevik Revolution, Russia was plunged into internal political crisis. Although **Lenin** and **Trotsky** hoped that 1917 would be a signal to workers throughout Europe to rise and overthrow their governments, the postwar revolutionary threat subsided, leaving Russia exposed and isolated.

Lenin (Vladimir Ulyanov) (1870–1924): Chairman of the Russian Social Democratic Party (Bolsheviks) and the most influential theoretical Marxist of his generation. He encouraged the party to launch the revolution in October 1917 and became the leader of the new government until illness in 1922 forced him to withdraw from active politics.

Trotsky, Leon (1879–1940): Russian socialist belonging to the Menshevik wing of the party. He became a Bolshevik in 1917 and commanded the Red Army during the Russian Civil War. He resigned in 1925 and was then accused of left-wing deviation, expelled from the party and sent into exile in 1929.

Its reduced weight in the international scales was confirmed by its defeat at Polish hands in 1920 when the Red Army tried to seize Warsaw. By 1925 most Bolshevik leaders had modified the effort to export communism and spoke instead of 'socialism in one country'. The Soviet Union deliberately cut itself off from the rest of the international system. The priority of the regime was to prevent war again on Russian soil and to avoid any diplomatic entanglements likely to bring such a risk about. There is no doubt that the Soviet Union possessed great potential strength, and that other powers underestimated the communists' ability to create a powerful military and economic state. But in the 1920s Russia no longer played the part in great-power calculations that it had done before 1914.

The same was true, though for very different reasons, of the United States. America had begun before 1914 to exert increasing influence on international affairs, particularly in the Pacific area. When, in 1917, **President Wilson** brought the United States into the war, and dominated the postwar peace settlement, it seemed that European power was destined to give way to American. Yet a year after the end of the war the United States turned its back on Europe. Congress refused to ratify the Versailles Treaty or to join the League of Nations. The mood of American public opinion was strongly isolationist. The feeling was widespread that the United States had been led into war by profiteers and bankers in order to shore up the French and British Empires, whose role in world affairs Americans deeply distrusted. Although there was no shortage of goodwill on the part of the United States, demonstrated in the efforts to resolve German financial difficulties in the 1923 **German inflation** crisis and again in 1931, the major priority of American foreign policy was to avoid fighting another war for Europe. Yet by the 1920s the United States had become the world's largest economy, backed up by vast material resources and a large population. Like the Soviet Union it possessed great potential military and economic strength, but chose, for domestic reasons, not to exert it in the international arena (Offner, 1975).

The source of American strength was economic power. Inexorably, with the onset of industrialization, there was a correlation between economic power and international influence. War itself was now industrialized. France and Britain were, in relative terms, declining economies. Britain's share of world trade in manufactured goods was 46 per cent in 1870, but was only 25 per cent by 1914. France's economic growth rate before 1914 was lower than Britain's, and only half that of Germany's. As new economies developed and grew, so the whole pattern of the international system was thrown into flux. Until economic potential was fully realized it was impossible to stabilize the system. America was a rising economic power which sooner or later would exercise its strength internationally. But so too were Japan, Germany and Italy. All three were new industrial economies, with high rates of growth.

Wilson, Woodrow (1856–1924): Democrat politician who became President of the United States from 1913 to 1921. He played a major part in shaping the postwar settlement in Europe with his insistence on 'self-determination', but the US Senate rejected the Versailles Settlement in 1920.

German inflation: The collapse of the German currency (the mark) in November 1923 following almost ten years of escalating inflation, chiefly caused by huge government borrowing during the war. The currency was stabilized in 1924 with international help, but a generation of German savers and investors was ruined.

Although German economic strength was temporarily broken in 1918, it rapidly revived so that by 1928 Germany was almost as economically powerful as it had been in 1914. By the 1920s, partly because of Britain's involvement in the war, Japan had become the major economy in east and south Asia. In Italy Mussolini's early years of rule coincided with a great upsurge in Italian trade and output. Sooner or later these states, too, like the United States and the Soviet Union, would have to be incorporated into the existing great-power system.

The very speed of these changes contributed to undermining the ability of the powers, any powers, to secure peace and social progress on their own terms. Within thirty or forty years the social structure and political systems of Europe and its imitators were transformed. Slow evolution was superseded by rapid change; the narrow political nation was replaced by mass politics which, in some cases, placed an intolerable strain on the existing political structure. In Germany and Italy it threw up new radical authoritarian movements hostile to the old order yet deeply distrustful of the modern 'liberal capitalism' borrowed from the model of western Europe. In Japan it touched off a militarist nationalism which sought to harness Japan's new economic strength to new political ambitions abroad. All these groups were infected with the ideology of imperialism and cultural superiority, whose manifestation in the form of British and French power they were committed to contest.

In the era of the two world wars, against a background of social and political transformation, international relations were in transition. Stability might have been achieved by concerted action based around a shared interest in securing peace as it had been in the nineteenth century, and many ordinary Europeans wished for nothing less after the shattering experience of the Great War. Or it might have been achieved through the existence of powers so strong that they could impose their will on the whole system, as was the case after 1945. But neither of these things happened. Instead there was a growing contradiction between the existing international system and the reality of power, made more dangerous by the restless political and ideological forces released by economic modernization and the rise of mass politics. These facts did not directly cause the war of 1939 or 1941, but they created an unstable context for the conduct of foreign affairs, and generated ambitions that made war more probable.

Part 2

ANALYSIS

2

The International Crisis

D uring the 1920s diplomacy was conducted against a background of relative international stability. The victor powers, Britain and France, played a dominant role, the one in Europe, the other outside it. The 1920s saw the heyday of liberal imperial politics and the peak of Franco-British influence. This reality was masked to some extent by their joint commitment to the League of Nations and the idea of collective security enshrined in the initial Covenant [**Doc. 2, p. 103**]. The effectiveness of the League as an instrument for genuine security was never severely tested in the 1920s, but the absence from its ranks of the United States and the Soviet Union and, until 1926, of Germany too, made the League a more fragile instrument than its architects had intended.

To underline the commitment to peace and to the rational, restrained pursuit of self-interest that it required, the powers sought firmer guarantees that would embody the spirit of the Covenant. In the 1922 Washington Treaty, Britain and Japan agreed with the non-League United States to limit their naval armaments and to guarantee the future security of China. The League itself sought positive ways to honour the undertaking to encourage general disarmament expressed in Article 8 of the Covenant, but not until 1932 did a **Disarmament Conference** finally convene at Geneva. In 1925 agreements were signed at Locarno in Switzerland between Britain, France, Germany, Italy and Belgium to guarantee the frontiers drawn up in the Versailles Treaty for western Europe. Unlike 1919, German leaders voluntarily acknowledged the loss of western territories – Alsace-Lorraine to France, Eupen and Malmédy to Belgium. On a pledge of further good behaviour, Germany was invited to join the League in 1926.

The final flourish of collaboration was made in Rome in June 1933 with a Four-Power-Pact (which was never ratified). Under the terms of the Pact Britain, France, Italy and Germany again reiterated their commitment to Locarno and the League by undertaking not to embark on destabilizing unilateral initiatives in Europe. The direct beneficiaries of all these initiatives

Disarmament Conference: Conference convoked through the auspices of the League of Nations in February 1932 under the chairmanship of the Labour politician Arthur Henderson. It failed to reach agreement on any measure of arms reduction and adjourned in October 1933 without reconvening.

were France and Britain, who were able to keep their worldwide imperial interests while maintaining the fiction of possible collective action – for fiction it turned out to be – to sustain the very stability needed to preserve those interests intact.

THE COLLAPSE OF THE LEAGUE

The first serious cracks in the 'liberal' diplomatic system were brought about by the collapse of the world economy in 1929. The world slump that followed encouraged the growth of protectionist, isolationist policies that exposed the weakness of collective action. As the major powers scrambled to protect their own economic interests, often at the expense of smaller and poorer economies, the spirit of co-operation and mutual aid evaporated. As the depression deepened the western powers cut back more sharply on military spending, which only served to weaken the international system still further. In Germany and Japan, countries hit particularly severely by the slump, domestic politics became dominated by radical nationalist groups which demanded an active foreign policy in order to help overcome economic difficulties, and to exploit the temporary inaction of the West as it tried to cope with the economic crisis.

The first challenge to the League was made by Japan when, in September 1931, its army invaded the Chinese province of Manchuria and set up there a puppet state, Manchukuo, under Japanese control. Japanese pressure on the Chinese state had grown throughout the 1920s. China was in political chaos following the end of Manchu rule in 1911. The government was faced with a revolutionary threat from Chinese communism, but was also weakened by provincial disunity and conflict between rival warlords. Given Chinese weaknesses, and the Japanese search for more secure economic outlets the Manchurian invasion seemed to Japanese military and political leaders to be a natural step. As it turned out, the risk had been well calculated. The Soviet Union was caught in the midst of the upheaval of rural collectivization and forced industrialization, and did little. The League proved unable to force one of its own members to renounce aggression, because it lacked the resources to do so other than moral pressure and the threat of economic sanctions. The latter were difficult to impose, not only because they excluded the United States, but because the major League powers were worried about the effect sanctions might have on their Asian trade and Far East security in general (Crowley, 1966).

In 1933 Japan left the League and effectively removed the Far East from the system of collective security. In 1934, in violation of international agreements to preserve an '**Open Door**' policy in China (to allow open and equal access to Chinese markets), the Japanese government announced the Amau Doctrine, a warning to other powers to regard China as Japan's sphere of influence and to abandon trade with the Chinese and the provision of technical aid to them. There is no doubt that Japanese leaders, spurred on at home by the military, were encouraged to go further after 1932 than they might otherwise have done because of the weak response from the major powers. Even the United States, architect of the 'Open Door' policy and naval limitations in the Pacific, hesitated to do anything that would alienate the Japanese. Neither Britain nor America was willing, in the difficult political climate of the early 1930s, to confront Japan militarily, and each suspected the other of trying to pass on the responsibility and cost of doing so (Louis, 1971).

The Manchurian crisis was critical in underlining the weakness of the League and the hollowness of the equilibrium which its supporters had established. The Chinese leader, **Chiang Kai-shek**, thought in 1932 that the Japanese invasion signalled 'the beginning of the Second World War', and expected a global conflict to break out by 1936 at the latest (Sun, 1993: 16). It was followed by a sharp deterioration in the international situation in Europe. In January 1933 Hitler was appointed German Chancellor. He led a party committed to treaty revision and to a reassertion of German influence. From being a power that worked within the League system, however grudgingly, Germany now set out to repudiate it. Hitler withdrew the German delegation from the Disarmament Conference and the League of Nations in October 1933. The western powers already knew of German 'secret rearmament' before 1933 but had not perceived it as a serious threat. Under Hitler rearmament assumed a different character. Though the western powers had only a hazy idea of Hitler's ultimate intentions, it was clear that German rearmament would be directed at some time to a revision of the territorial settlement arranged at Versailles. This was not, as yet, a serious problem. The British, for their part, were not averse to some readjustment, provided it was achieved on British terms. But it did resurrect in a very direct way the threat that German power had posed to western interests before 1914. Britain and France were forced to look for ways in which Germany could be accommodated within the existing system without destroying its stability.

The rise of Hitler affected not only the western democracies but also Italy, where fascism had come to power a decade before. Italy had been accommodated into League diplomacy. If Mussolini was still not taken quite seriously by western statesmen, he took himself seriously enough. Italy played a major part in the search for collective guarantees and by the early 1930s had acquired through dint of Mussolini's efforts a considerable increase in diplomatic stature and military strength. A powerful Germany threatened to undo

Open-door policy: A system in which all states can trade on the basis of the same 'open' access to another market. The term is usually used to describe efforts to trade on equal terms with China.

Chiang Kai-shek (1887–1965): Chinese army officer who rose to power in China in the 1920s and fought a long civil war against Chinese communists and native warlords. He led Chinese resistance to Japanese invasion in the 1930s and 1940s but was defeated by communist insurgents in 1949.

some of these gains and to reduce Italian influence in central and south-eastern Europe. It is likely that this was the final factor that pushed Mussolini towards a policy of active imperialism in Africa and the beginning of an aggressive Mediterranean policy. Mussolini did not want to play the role of junior dictator to Hitler. As a result he brought Italy, in its turn, to a point where it could challenge the fragile balance of power.

Mussolini's imperialism had other roots as well, even though its emergence depended on diplomatic circumstances in Europe. Italian fascism was preoccupied with ideas of an Italian mission to reconstruct the fallen Roman Empire. This vision drew upon the prewar anti-Slav and colonialist traditions, which helps to explain Mussolini's interest in the Balkans, and in east and north Africa. He looked in particular at Ethiopia (Abyssinia), the only major independent state left in Africa. Links with Ethiopia were of long standing.

In 1923 Italy, against British and French objections, sponsored Ethiopia's membership of the League. An agreement for friendship had been signed in 1928, and Italy's economic and military influence in the area had been tacitly acknowledged by the other major colonial powers, a fact that persuaded Mussolini that they would not object on grounds of principle to the extension of formal Italian control over the country. In September 1933 he made the first public announcement that Italy would be seeking an outlet in Africa and Asia. A war plan for the attack on Ethiopia was drawn up in the summer of 1934 and in December he began active preparations for a campaign in the following autumn. In order to pre-empt possible retaliation from his League partners, Mussolini made efforts to create a favourable diplomatic situation which would ensure the success of his venture. In January 1935 he secured veiled agreement from the French Prime Minister, Pierre Laval. He hoped that Britain, too, would not be averse to Italian intervention, or could be restrained by France if it were, or would be frightened into acceptance by the military threat that Italy's Libyan armies posed to Egypt. To make this threat a possibility the Italian military began planning for a possible war against Britain to turn north and east Africa into an Italian imperial area at some future date.

On 3 October 1935 Italian forces invaded Ethiopia. Mussolini knew that it was a risk and hoped for a rapid victory. Although Italian aviators resorted to using gas bombs for the first time, the struggle, though unequal, was not straightforward. Not until 9 May 1936 was victory finally declared, but a violent pacification campaign continued thereafter. Mussolini failed in his gamble to create diplomatic approval of the Italian attack. The League rallied to Ethiopia's support, condemned the invasion, and invoked economic sanctions and an arms embargo against Italy. But in reality the invasion of Ethiopia could not be reversed any more than Manchuria. Britain and France came close to giving a limited approval by suggesting a compromise that would give Italy guaranteed influence in a still-independent Ethiopia (the so-called Hoare-Laval Pact, named after the British and French Foreign Ministers who negotiated it). When news of the Pact leaked out, the British and French governments both repudiated it and tried to show that they were enthusiastic about **sanctions**. The effect was to drive Italy much closer to Hitler's Germany, and make it increasingly hostile to Britain and France for obstructing the creation of an Italian empire, while sanctions broke down, as they had done in the case of Manchuria, because the United States, Japan and Germany were all outside the League. To the dismay of the smaller members, the major League states were not prepared to risk anything greater than protest, and in 1937 Italy followed Germany and Japan by withdrawing from the League altogether.

Sanctions: The policy of imposing an economic and financial boycott against states engaged in aggressive war in violation of the Covenant of the League of Nations. It was applied only to Italy during the Italo-Ethiopian War.

If Manchuria had begun the decline of the League system, Ethiopia brought about its eclipse. Sensing opportunities for gain, Japan and Italy tested the system to see what could be extracted. Collective security evaporated, demonstrating the extent to which it had always rested on the willingness and capacity of Britain and France to enforce it. Instead, both the major western powers pursued their own interests, unwilling and unable to prevent a serious challenge to the stability and security of the international system. By 1936 the League strategy was bankrupt; confidence in the British and French claims to moral ascendancy in world affairs was, with some justice, at a low ebb. The Disarmament Conference, which the major powers had used as evidence of their good intentions, broke up without serious achievement in June 1934 and was not reconvened. The Ethiopian crisis opened up the way to rearmament and provoked the first murmurings of general war.

FRANCE AND BRITAIN

Britain and France were now faced with the question of how to respond to the deterioration in the international situation. There was never any doubt that some sort of response was called for. Neither power was prepared to abandon its influence, prestige and safety. Yet neither possessed sufficient strength, either military or economic, to assert that influence decisively when challenged. Both powers were confronted by the central dilemma of having to defend large and geographically dispersed empires with relatively shrinking resources. 'We are a very rich and very vulnerable Empire,' wrote Neville Chamberlain, 'and there are plenty of poor adventurers not very far away who look upon us with hungry eyes' (Pratt, 1975: 198). Both British and

French strategy was greatly complicated by the global nature of their concerns. Where Germany, Italy and Japan could concentrate their efforts at revision in geographically distinct regions, the two western powers were compelled to adopt a worldwide strategy.

It was only this shared threat that pushed Britain and France closer together in the 1930s. Certainly until 1933 Britain was wary of French ambitions, while the French were disappointed at the way in which Britain had withdrawn from direct involvement in Europe at the end of the war. There were other reasons for cool relations. Britain was unfriendly towards French imperial ambitions in the Middle East and was not averse to some sort of colonial settlement with Germany. France, in turn, had proved unco-operative during the economic crisis and was held to bear much of the blame for the collapse of the international credit system in 1931.

A year later Robert Vansittart, Permanent Secretary at the British Foreign Office, complained that France had 'virtually attained the very thing that we have traditionally sought to avoid in Europe, hegemony, if not dictatorship, political and financial' (Reynolds, 1991: 118). Chamberlain's private view was that France 'never can keep a secret for more than half an hour, nor a government for more than nine months' (Feiling, 1946: 322). Until 1939 the British remained sceptical of France's value as an ally. The growing threat of Germany overcame some of these differences, but only on basic questions of the balance of power in Europe were there broad areas of agreement.

Yet even here the strategy that each adopted in the face of the German threat was very different. Both drew conclusions from the experience of 1914. The French, in the absence of an enforceable collective security, looked towards a system of firm alliances to restrain Germany. Britain wished to avoid at all costs the sort of alliance entanglements that were held to have brought about the First World War and adopted an increasingly isolationist outlook. Since France needed British support against Germany, the two strategies were clearly incompatible. In the end Britain was able to avoid any clear commitment to France until 1939, so that it was British strategy that tended to prevail, though France was never in any sense an entirely dependent or pliant instrument in British diplomacy as has often been suggested.

French strategy was based on one major consideration: the need to find firm guarantees for security in the event of the revival of German power. Yet conditions for an alliance system were very different from those in 1914. Real guarantees for security could only be found in a formal military commitment to France by Britain, which was not forthcoming until February 1939. The other option was to work for a two-front containment of Germany. Following this strategy France established a network of alliances, some of them carrying military agreements as well, with the new states of eastern Europe. Agreement was reached with Poland in 1921, Czechoslovakia in 1924,

Romania in 1926 and Yugoslavia in 1927. The so-called Little Entente in central Europe was intended to play the role that the Franco-Russian alliance had filled before 1914 (Adamthwaite, 1995; Young, 1996). But such a relationship was fraught with problems. The promises of military aid were ambiguous, since France could clearly offer little immediate help in the event of a German thrust eastwards. Nor could the eastern states be relied on to agree among themselves sufficiently to restrain Germany with any effect. In 1935 France tried to secure a firmer base in the east by reaching an agreement with the Soviet Union, but this only served to alienate the smaller eastern powers from France while it provided no firm guarantee of any kind of Soviet action against Germany. To make things worse Belgium in 1936 overturned the military agreement of 1920 to co-operate with France, removing an important defensive line against Germany. Nor could Italy, once Mussolini had embarked on a Mediterranean strategy hostile to French interests, be used as a diplomatic make-weight to restrain German moves in central Europe, as had been hoped.

The French were finally compelled by circumstances to follow British strategy. The coming to power of the **Popular Front** of centre-left parties in 1936 made this easier for it marked a shift away from support for the League and collective action, on which French foreign policy still formally rested, to a more active search for alternative ways of containing or accommodating German ambitions and the threat posed by European fascism. British strategy was based on a clear conviction that firm alliances were a diplomatic liability and that all powers could be won over by adopting a flexible and pragmatic approach to problems as they arose. This conviction survived until 1939. Until then Britain avoided fixed commitments, particularly to France or to the countries of central and south-eastern Europe, while making spasmodic attempts to win over potential enemies by policies which the British regarded as realistic and reasonable. Third parties were used to bring pressure to bear, when needed, on other powers. Great weight was placed upon Britain's commitment to international morality. If such a strategy appeared to Britain's friends to border on incoherence, to Britain's leaders it resembled a gigantic and increasingly dangerous game of chess.

The key element in the game was to maintain what Chamberlain called a 'balance of risks'. Too firm a commitment in one part of the globe might disturb the balance in another. At all costs Britain had to avoid a simultaneous challenge in the areas of key strategic importance, in Europe, the Mediterranean and India. The Defence Requirements Committee report in 1935 summed up this principle: 'It is a cardinal requirement of our national and Imperial security that our foreign policy should be so conducted as to avoid the possible development of a situation in which we might be confronted simultaneously with the hostility of Japan in the Far East, Germany

Popular Front: Term used in 1935 to describe the political alliance between progressive political forces, principally social-democrats and communists, to combat the threat of fascism. It is usually applied to the French government elected in 1935 and the Spanish government elected in 1936.

in the West and any power on the main line of communications between the two' (Mommsen and Kettenacker, 1983: 176). When Chamberlain became Prime Minister in 1937 he adopted this principle as his own.

The word that British statesmen chose to describe this response was 'appeasement'. It was an unfortunate choice, for it came to imply a weak and fearful policy of concession to potential aggressors. In fact appeasement was far from that. It was more or less consistent with the main lines of British foreign policy going back into the nineteenth century. It was used to describe British policy towards Germany in the 1920s, which was regarded then as sensible and statesmanlike. It was employed later with the Soviet Union during the war, when it was hailed by the public as sound politics. By appeasement was meant a policy of adjustment and accommodation of conflicting interests broadly to conform with Britain's unique position in world affairs. It involved no preconceived plan of action, but rested on a number of political and moral assumptions about the virtue of compromise and peaceableness, which suited Britain's economic and imperial interests very well. It involved using the instruments of British power – trading and financial strength, and a wealth of diplomatic experience – to their fullest advantage. But it also implied that there were limits to British policy beyond which other powers should not be permitted to go. Appeasement was an acceptable strategy only as long as it matched what were perceived to be British interests. Chamberlain saw himself as part of this tradition. When he became Prime Minister in May 1937 he assumed much more responsibility for foreign affairs than had his predecessor **Stanley Baldwin**, hoping to be able to produce what he called a '**Grand Settlement**' of international problems through a concert orchestrated by Britain (Parker, 1993).

Seen from the perspective of British foreign policy, the initial reaction towards aggression and the breakdown of collective security makes much more sense. Britain sought to treat problems as they arose, on their merits, but within certain loosely defined parameters. In the Far East, for example, the British were prepared to accommodate Japanese ambitions, but only up to a point. It was recognized that Japan had a natural sphere of influence in northern China. It was hoped that Japan would counter the threat posed to India by the Soviet Union, and that Japan would become so embroiled in the problems of ruling Manchuria that it would no longer pose such a danger to peace. But acceptance of Japan's special position in the north was made only on the basis that Japan would respect the special privileges enjoyed by British trade and British officials throughout China (Louis, 1971). There were similar limits to Britain's appeasement of Italy. Some African and colonial readjustment was thought desirable throughout the 1930s. While condemning Italy at the League, Britain continued to search for ways of repartitioning Africa, possibly by using Portugal's colonies as bargaining counters. The Italian conquest

Appeasement: British and French attempts to satisfy or 'appease' the demands of aggressor nations during the 1930s.

Baldwin, Stanley (1867–1947): Conservative politician who became Chancellor of the Exchequer in 1922 and was Prime Minister 1922–4 and 1924–9. He joined Ramsay MacDonald's National Government in 1931 as Lord President of the Council and Deputy Prime Minister, and became Prime Minister again from 1935 to his retirement in 1937.

Grand Settlement: Term used by Neville Chamberlain to describe a multilateral negotiated settlement of all outstanding issues of frontiers, minorities, access to markets and raw materials, replacing the Versailles Settlement of 1919.

of Ethiopia was not a vital concern to Britain, but the Italian threat to Egypt and Malta was. During 1936 and 1937 the British made efforts to drive a wedge between Hitler and Mussolini in the hope of making Italy more dependent on British and French goodwill. But at the same time both the western powers made it clear that continued Italian hostility was not to be tolerated and would be contained in Africa and in the Mediterranean in the absence of a reasonable settlement. The result was unfortunate in both cases, for appeasement, rather than satisfying Italy and Japan, pushed them closer to Germany (Pratt, 1975).

With Germany the situation was altogether more delicate. Accommodation of German demands meant tearing up the Versailles Settlement. This was less of a problem for Britain than for France. Many British politicians had been unhappy with the treaty from the outset and had already made moves to conciliate Germany before Hitler came to power. The feeling was widespread that German grievances were, up to a point, justified and that a lasting peace could only be secured by removing the more vindictive aspects of the peace settlement. If someone other than Hitler had led Germany in the 1930s, much of the Versailles Settlement might have been abandoned through mutual agreement. The most contentious issue in the 1920s had been the German payment of **reparations** to the Allies for war damage. The annual payments were negotiated down in 1924 and again in 1929. At the Lausanne Conference in 1932 they were suspended indefinitely. Britain turned a blind eye to limited German rearmament beyond the levels laid down in 1919, and in 1935 signed an Anglo-German Naval Agreement which acknowledged Germany's right to build naval forces well beyond what had been permitted, but within limits acceptable to the British Admiralty. When Hitler publicly declared German rearmament in the same year there was little protest. During the 1930s the British government toyed with the idea of returning some, though not all, German colonies which had been taken over by the Allies in 1919 [**Doc. 3, p. 103**]. None of this was deemed to pose an immediate threat to British interests, and if it left German leaders satiated, so much the better. The French were understandably more anxious about making any concessions to Germany, partly because reparations were of real economic value to France, partly because the long common frontier with Germany made French security a more pressing issue than British.

Rightly or wrongly, British statesmen saw Germany as a power which, treated with respect and good sense, could be brought back into the great-power system without destroying it. There were plenty of warnings, from a wide variety of official and unofficial sources, that Hitler's ambitions were without limit, unpredictable and dangerous. With the benefit of hindsight we now know this to be true. But certainly until 1938 Hitler asked for nothing that the British were not, in the end, willing to grant. The British government

Reparations: Payments in kind and money demanded by the victorious Allies in 1919 from Germany and its allies. Reparations were paid by Bulgaria, Hungary, and Austria, but the bulk were extracted from Germany, who continued to pay them until 1932 when economic crisis forced a moratorium.

was not prepared to give Germany a free hand in eastern Europe, or the right to tear up the Versailles Settlement on its own terms. Concessions to Germany were made in the knowledge that they fitted in with a realistic appraisal of British interests, even though they trampled on the interests of lesser powers. But they were made on what the British saw as their terms. Only when Hitler refused to accept this framework did the British state clearly, in 1939, the limits of their policy. Until then the British worked on the assumption expressed by **Lord Halifax**, that there was room for a 'possible alteration in the European order' (Newman, 1976: 29).

The problem was that appeasement, in order to be successful, had to be conducted from a position of some strength. Instead, the two western states found themselves offering concessions from a position of relative weakness. In the first place neither was sufficiently well-armed in the early 1930s to meet force with force without running the risk of weakening, perhaps fatally, its global interests. The pursuit of appeasement was therefore necessary to buy time for rearmament. Then there were problems in domestic politics. There was strong pressure from pacifist opinion in both Britain and France to avoid any confrontation that might involve war. This pressure was underlined by the fear of bombing, shared by government and public alike. With the onset of air rearmament governments everywhere were encouraged to be more circumspect in international affairs, not realizing as historians now do, that there were profound limitations of a technical kind which would have made it impossible for any power to launch a successful bombing offensive in the 1930s against enemy cities (Bialer, 1980).

There was also evidence of growing ideological conflict. British and French governments were as frightened of communism as of fascism in the mid-1930s. Certainly in Britain elements among the traditional ruling class were not unsympathetic to Hitler and Mussolini, whereas they were deeply hostile to communism. **Sir Alexander Cadogan** at the Foreign Office feared that 'war may place the whole of Europe at the mercy of Russia' (Gladwyn, 1972: 84). This ambiguous assessment of fascism explains the muted response of the western powers to the outbreak of civil war in Spain in 1936. Neither state would give aid to the democratic and socialist forces fighting to preserve the recently founded Spanish republic. 'In the present state of Europe,' argued the Cabinet Secretary, **Sir Maurice Hankey**, 'with France and Spain menaced by Bolshevism, it is not inconceivable that before long it might pay us to throw in our lot with Germany and Italy' (Newman, 1976: 39). Even by 1938 it was not clear exactly what sort of threat fascism posed, but the threat presented by communism had been made clear in October 1917. There were real doubts in conservative circles about whether or not the British and French working classes would support a more active foreign policy which might be interpreted as another 'capitalist war'. In France, after

---

Halifax, Lord Edward (1881–1959): Senior Conservative politician, who was Viceroy to India 1926–31 and then became Foreign Secretary in 1938 following Eden's resignation. He favoured limited appeasement and was replaced as Foreign Secretary by Eden late in 1940. He was posted to Washington as British Ambassador 1941–6.

Cadogan, Alexander (1884–1968): Permanent Under-Secretary at the British Foreign Office from 1938 to 1945, and Britain's representative at the United Nations between 1946 and 1950.

Hankey, Maurice (1877–1963): Long-serving Secretary to the Committee for Imperial Defence from 1912–1938 and British Cabinet Secretary from 1916 to 1938. He was appointed to Chamberlain's war cabinet in 1939, but excluded when Churchill became Prime Minister.

the fall of the Popular Front in 1938, some right-wing groups favoured closer collaboration with Hitler as the only way of preventing the eventual bolshevization of western Europe.

AMERICA AND THE SOVIET UNION

All of these factors – military weakness, fear of war, ideological and political tensions – had to be weighed in the balance when assessing foreign policy. They seemed to confirm the wisdom of adopting a conciliatory stand and the dangers of a more confrontational or bellicose strategy. But there were other, more imponderable elements in the international system which contributed to the general climate of uncertainty. This was particularly the case with the attitude of the United States and the Soviet Union to the growing international crisis.

United States foreign policy, according to **Cordell Hull**, Roosevelt's Secretary of State, could be summed up in one phrase: 'keeping this country out of war'. Americans had been deeply affected by the experience of intervention in the First World War which they came to see as an unnecessary sacrifice on behalf of an ungrateful Europe. Throughout the interwar years American governments avoided making commitments of any kind in Europe for fear that they would be dragged into conflict. This determination to avoid an active foreign policy was strengthened in the years of economic depression, when Roosevelt's economic recovery programme, the '**New Deal**', took priority. Roosevelt hesitated to do anything abroad in case the powerful isolationist lobby undermined his domestic programme. To buy agreement at home the American government turned away from world affairs. Some isolationists wished to go even further than this. In 1935 they introduced a temporary Neutrality Act in Congress which became law in August, forbidding the granting of loans or the sale of arms to any belligerent. In January 1937 the act was extended to civil war in order to prevent the sale of arms to Spain, and on 1 May 1937 a permanent Neutrality Act was signed by Roosevelt which differed from the original act in that it allowed belligerents to fetch only non-war supplies from the United States in their own ships, for cash.

The strong desire for neutrality was matched by a general desire for appeasement [**Doc. 4, p. 104**]. American statesmen were convinced that the key to world peace lay in the recovery of the world economy. 'The truth is universally recognised,' said Hull, 'that trade between nations is the greatest peacemaker and civiliser within human experience': a healthy economy would allow 'settlement among nations of any political questions' (Schatz, 1970–1: 86). Roosevelt played with the idea of a major conference to thrash all such questions out, which looked very much like Chamberlain's 'Grand

Hull, Cordell (1871–1955): American Democrat politician who became Roosevelt's Secretary of State from 1932 until 1944. He was committed to the belief that all conflicts have economic causes and that worldwide prosperity would bring peace. He was awarded the Nobel peace prize in 1945.

New Deal: Package of economic and welfare policies instituted by President Roosevelt in 1933–4 following his election, to try to cope with the social consequences of the slump.

Settlement'. But beyond vague pronouncements on the need for collective action and expressions of peace and goodwill, the American government did very little. In the Far East Japan was able to overturn the 'Open Door' with scant American resistance. When American ships were attacked by Japanese aircraft in China in December 1937 Roosevelt accepted a grudging Japanese apology but took no action. In Europe the United States, while clearly more sympathetic to the democracies than to the dictatorships, avoided open commitments. It was with deep regret that Roosevelt observed the gradual breakdown of the League system. Though he was willing to condemn aggression, as he did in his 'quarantine' speech on 5 October 1937, he remained committed to the idea that economic concessions and a deep respect for international morality were the necessary instruments for the proper conduct of world affairs (Divine, 1965).

The American attitude was also born of a deep distrust of British and French motives, which had taken root at Versailles when both powers scrambled for the imperial spoils from defeated Germany. American leaders could not rid themselves of the suspicion that Britain hoped to use American power, as in 1917, to rescue the British Empire from collapse. The perception was widely held in America that Britain was still the dominant global power, and the Americans expected Britain to accept the responsibility that dominance entailed (McKercher, 1991). In the Far East both powers played a complex game to avoid having to take the lead in confronting Japan. In November 1937 Roosevelt urged that America should not 'be pushed out in front as the leader in, or suggester of, future action' (Offner, 1975: 151) and he hoped Britain would do more. This unfavourable view of Britain was confirmed by what Americans saw as Britain's unwillingness to make substantial efforts to restore free trade in its empire as a key to securing a more general economic settlement. American interests seemed more likely to be served by a general loosening of empire ties, a view that ran directly counter to the interests of the two major imperial powers.

Britain, on the other hand, stood to gain a great deal from American support, yet could never be certain if any would be forthcoming. Chamberlain despaired of American foreign policy: 'It is always best and safest to count on nothing from the Americans except words' (Preston, 1978: 120). The neutrality legislation brought the prospect for Britain and France that it might encourage further acts of aggression by hostile powers. But attempts to lure the United States into underpinning western strategy failed at every turn before 1939. Roosevelt was, by 1938, thoroughly disillusioned with Europe, where no one gave 'a continental damn what the United States thinks or does' (Schmitz and Challener, 1990: 6). Nor, in the end, did Britain pursue such attempts with much determination, because of the danger that too great a dependence on the United States would reduce British influence and might involve substantial concessions on trade and colonial self-government. American help on these terms would be a very mixed blessing.

The same uncertainty and ambiguity characterized the attitude of the west to the Soviet Union. Soviet friendship, despite repeated assurances of its peaceful intentions, could not be counted upon. In Soviet propaganda the British Empire was portrayed as the major enemy of the Soviet state. France had closer ties, and a greater interest in winning Soviet co-operation. But the pact signed in 1935 between the two countries was never effectively extended to a military commitment, and after the fall of the Popular Front and with the decline of the French economy, Soviet leaders lost interest in French support. Soviet strategy was similar to that of the United States: a strong desire to avoid war at all costs; a commitment to collective action for peace; and a strong suspicion that the western European powers merely regarded the USSR as an instrument in their efforts to preserve world capitalism [**Doc. 5, p. 104**]. Like America, Russia wished to avoid any binding commitment. Though Russia had little confidence in the League of Nations, to which it was admitted in 1934, its Foreign Minister preferred it to a strategy of 'military alliance and the balance of power' which 'not only does not get rid of war, but on the contrary unleashes it' (Ulam, 1968: 218). Formal, collective action through the League reduced the danger that the USSR might be isolated by the capitalist powers. Soviet leaders rightly saw the greatest direct threat coming from Germany and Japan, but they did not as a result draw closer to Britain and France, partly from fear of alienating Germany and Japan still further, partly from a belief that the western powers were facing serious economic crisis and could not be trusted to honour any bargain struck. Until 1939, when the Soviet Union found itself in the fortuitous position of being wooed by both sides, it kept out of the international arena. The European powers, for their part, while aware that the Soviet Union might at some stage play a vital part in the balance of power, believed that Stalin's industrialization drive, and the savage **purges** that followed it, rendered it incapable of playing a full part in international affairs for the foreseeable future. Soviet weakness, like American neutrality, made it harder to restrain Germany and Japan, though for the British and French it postponed the day when communism might threaten the existing order (Ulam, 1968: 72).

Soviet purges: Term loosely used to describe the period 1936–8 when almost 700,000 were executed by the Soviet judicial system for alleged crimes against the state. The victims included many Communist Party leaders and a high proportion of the leadership of the army and navy.

FROM THE RHINELAND TO MUNICH

American neutrality and Soviet isolation did indeed carry the danger that Germany, Italy and Japan would be encouraged to pursue an adventurous foreign policy. So, too, did appeasement, which was interpreted not as great-power magnanimity but as a sign of weakness and moral decay. Once it became clear that the western powers would not take firm action, and indeed were willing to be conciliatory, the challenge to the existing system was rapidly extended. The three revisionist states were united in their rejection of the framework within which Anglo-French diplomacy was conducted. They saw mere arrogance in claims that could not be backed up by force. The slow pace of western rearmament and the constraints evidently imposed by domestic political and economic considerations all appeared to show that here were empires in decline, decadent plutocracies whose course was run. Though they eschewed any formal alliance, the three powers recognized their mutual interests by establishing an informal diplomatic 'axis'. In November 1936 Germany and Japan signed the Anti-**Comintern** Pact which committed them to co-operate in some unspecified way to contain the threat of international communism. Italy joined the Pact one year later. From that point the rest of the world, rightly or wrongly, came to see the three 'axis' states as linked by a common interest in revising the existing international political order.

From 1936 onwards the crisis of that international order could no longer be disguised. On 15 March 1936 German troops entered the demilitarized zone of the Rhineland and re-established a common military frontier with France once again. The other states did nothing, distracted by the Ethiopian affair, and unconvinced that their populations would see the Rhineland as an issue remotely worth contesting (though many historians have since argued, with calculated hindsight, that this was the point when Hitler should have been restrained by force). Later in the year Hitler ordered an acceleration in German rearmament, and the establishment of an economy geared to Germany's long-term military requirements. In July civil war broke out in Spain between rebel nationalists, led by General Francisco Franco, and socialist and liberal forces loyal to the Spanish Second Republic, founded in 1931. Mussolini, fresh from victory in Ethiopia, sent Italian forces and supplies to help Franco. Hitler was persuaded to send a limited number of German military advisers and a small air force, the **Condor Legion**. Britain and France organized a **Non-Intervention** Committee to try to enforce an international neutrality in the Spanish war. Twenty-seven states joined the committee, including Italy and Germany who openly flouted the agreement. The decision by the Soviet government to send help to the loyalist side turned the civil war into a symbolic conflict between fascism, communism and democracy.

The **Spanish Civil War** had significant international implications. It unwittingly created the battlelines of the future world war. It brought Britain and France together and laid the foundations for their co-operation over the next three years. The war weakened French ability to act forcefully elsewhere in Europe, because of the fear that an authoritarian pro-fascist regime would

Comintern: The Third International of communists, set up by Lenin in 1919 to succeed the defunct Second International. It became an instrument for Soviet control of other communist parties and was wound up in 1943.

Condor Legion: A unit of several thousand German airmen sent to Spain in 1936 to assist Franco's rebellion against the republican government. Commanded by Werner von Richthofen, the Legion was notorious for the bombing of the Basque city of Guernica on 26 April 1937.

Non-Intervention: Agreement reached between all the major states in late 1936 not to intervene militarily in the Spanish Civil War. Only Britain and France observed the agreement. Italy, Germany and the Soviet Union all gave aid to one side or the other.

Spanish Civil War: Conflict between rebel nationalist forces led by General Franco and the armed forces and irregular socialist and anarchist militia in support of the Spanish Second Republic. The nationalist revolt began in July 1936 and ended with Franco's victory in March 1939.

triumph in Madrid, leaving France surrounded on three frontiers by hostile powers. The war also led to a growing rift between Italy and the western states, which pushed Mussolini, now keen to transcend the existing European order, closer to Hitler (Frank, 1987). German-Italian friendship offered Hitler the opportunity to act more forcefully in central Europe, which until 1937 Italy had regarded as a vital area for Italian security. On 5 November 1937 Hitler called together senior military and diplomatic personnel to brief them on how he saw German foreign policy unfolding [**Doc. 6, p. 105**]. His immediate aim was to unite Austria – a rump German state created out of the ruins of the Habsburg Empire in 1918 – with the new German Reich, and to dismember Czechoslovakia, in order to bring under German rule the three million German speakers living within its frontiers. With Britain and France manifestly unwilling to intervene actively in European affairs, and with Italian acquiescence, Hitler told his audience that action might be possible soon. On 12 March 1938, on the grounds that internal political conflict made Austria ungovernable (the conflict was largely fuelled by the Austrian National Socialist Party), German troops occupied Vienna and the union, *Anschluss*, of the two countries was proclaimed the following day. There were no international complications.

Anschluss: Literally the 'joining on' of Austria to Germany after German troops occupied the country on 12 March 1938.

In the Far East the crisis intensified in the summer of 1937. Between 1932 and 1937 Japan continued to exert pressure on Chinese interests in northern China. There were numerous small conflicts but no open war. In 1936 the Chinese leader, Chiang Kai-shek, was divided between his desire to drive back Japanese encroachment and his need to create domestic political stability. A prolonged civil war with the Chinese communists and regional military warlords enfeebled China's capacity to confront the common Japanese enemy. In September 1936 Japan demanded a Japanese-controlled buffer zone in northern China. Chiang rejected the demand and began to search for international support for Chinese resistance. No formal alliance was forthcoming, despite wide public sympathy abroad for China's plight, particularly in the United States. During the course of 1937 Chiang was able to cement greater domestic unity and was persuaded to abandon the anti-communist war for long enough to confront Japan. In July 1937 a violent incident near Beijing (Peking) escalated into a serious military confrontation. In August Chiang decided on all-out war with Japan. The consequences were disastrous. Japanese leaders used Chinese resistance as the excuse for further imperialism. In December 1937 Chiang's capital at Nanking fell to Japan amidst scenes of appalling barbarity, and China faced a long-drawn out war (Sun, 1993).

All of this made appeasement look increasingly hollow. The international order was disintegrating. Warfare, somewhere, was now a permanent feature. For Britain and France the balance between conciliation and containment became severely strained. Even Chamberlain, who so hoped to orchestrate a lasting peace, came to see as early as the spring of 1938 that 'force is the only argument Germany understands' (Dilks, 1971: 81). Both states were confronted with the stark paradox that the more they sought settlement and reconciliation, the more rapidly they created the conditions that made reconciliation impossible. Nevertheless, Chamberlain clung to the view that appeasement, once properly understood, could still bring about an international settlement on British terms. During the summer of 1938 the issue of Czechoslovakia, placed on Hitler's own agenda the previous November, became the testing point of Chamberlain's 'Grand Settlement'.

This was certainly not the British intention. British politicians were detached from the problems of eastern Europe, a region that had been dominated for years by French security interests. The issue of German irredentism in Czechoslovakia became a British concern largely because of Chamberlain's fear that French support for the Czechs in any confrontation with Germany might plunge Europe unnecessarily into war. The British view on the future of the **Sudeten Germans** was a sympathetic one. In 1937 there had been hints from London that the Sudeten question might be included in a general settlement of European issues. In March 1938 the British cabinet agreed that no military help would be forthcoming to preserve the Czech state, and that if it became necessary the Czech government would be pressured to make concessions on what was clearly, in Churchill's words, 'an affront to self-determination' (Howard, 1972: 121). There was widespread agreement with the judgement of the permanent head of the Foreign Office, Alexander Cadogan, that the Czech issue was not one 'on which we should be on very strong ground for plunging Europe into war' (Newman, 1976: 33–4). What the British, and the French, would not tolerate was a unilateral effort by Germany to alter the political settlement in Czechoslovakia by force.

This was precisely what Hitler had in mind. Shortly after the *Anschluss* the German press began a campaign of propaganda against Czechoslovakia, the 'inconceivable creation' as **Goering** called it. While the German press stridently demanded the return of the Sudetenland, Hitler privately planned for the destruction of Czechoslovakia. On 28 May he announced to generals and ministers his intention of smashing the Czech state in the near future. There was, he assured them, 'no danger of a preventive war by foreign states against Germany' (Overy, 1998: 47). The military were ordered to plan a short campaign in the autumn, while the Sudeten Germans were encouraged to make unacceptable demands to ensure that war would be the result. Hitler expected to be able to isolate the Czechs, and then present his public with a short and glorious conflict.

Hitler was right to see that the survival of Czech rule over three million ethnic Germans was not a situation that either Britain or France would be

Sudeten Germans: German-speaking population of northern Bohemia who were placed under Czechoslovak rule in 1919 when the Habsburg Empire was formally partitioned in the Versailles Settlement.

Goering, Marshal Hermann (1893–1946): Joined the National Socialist Party in 1922 and rose to be one its senior politicians. In 1932 he was President of the Reichstag and in 1935 was made Commander-in-Chief of the German air force. He committed suicide at Nuremberg in 1946 after being condemned to death for war crimes.

prepared to defend. But the Czech issue refused to remain localized because it involved the only remaining democracy in eastern Europe to which France had made earlier pledges of support. On the weekend of 20–1 May the Czech government ordered a partial mobilization in the belief that German action might be imminent. The so-called 'Weekend Crisis', which was a false alarm, alerted Britain and France to the seriousness of the issue, and both put pressure on the Czech President, **Edouard Beneš**, to make concessions to the Sudeten Germans, even to contemplate their cession to Germany. On 3 August Britain backed an international commission, headed by the veteran British politician, Lord Runciman, to travel to Czechoslovakia and investigate the situation. His commission recommended some form of autonomy, and on 18 August Beneš, with very little room for manoeuvre, agreed to make substantial concessions to the German position.

The concessions were rejected in Berlin while Hitler pressed on with the plan to attack Czechoslovakia in the late autumn. Britain and France faced the sudden prospect of a choice between a humiliating climb-down and war, the very worst outcome from Chamberlain's efforts for peace. On 15 September Chamberlain took the decision to fly to Germany to confront Hitler face-to-face. Flattered by Chamberlain's attention – it was the British Prime Minister's first flight in an aeroplane – Hitler agreed to engage in negotiations over the Sudetenland and to stand back from invasion. It was an elaborate bluff. When Chamberlain returned to Germany on 22 September to discuss the details of the settlement Hitler presented him with an ultimatum: the Sudeten areas would be handed over by 28 September or Germany would use force. After heated argument Hitler altered the date to 1 October.

Chamberlain returned to London with the prospect of war looming. He wanted to avoid a general conflict at all costs, but his cabinet would not accept an ultimatum. There were divisions of opinion in Paris too, but Prime Minister **Edouard Daladier** would not bow to the open threat of force. Both governments ordered mobilization preparations [**Doc. 7, p. 106**]. By 27 September both Britain and France were formally committed to defend Czech sovereignty by force if German troops crossed the frontier without agreement. On the 26th Chamberlain sent his personal emissary, Sir Horace Wilson, to confront Hitler. He told the dictator that if Germany attacked Czechoslovakia, France would honour its commitment and that Britain would then support France. German forces were due to march the following day, but, faced with the risk of a major war, Hitler backed down. On 28 September Mussolini, at British prompting, interceded to suggest a four-power conference over the Sudeten affair and Hitler, in ill temper, accepted the idea. Though the crisis is usually represented as one in which Chamberlain cravenly gave in to Hitler, it was Hitler who gave way to the west at the last moment because he was not yet ready for a European conflict.

Beneš, Edouard (1884–1948): Czech politician who was Foreign Minister from 1918 to 1935, then President, following the death of Thomas Masaryk. He left Czechoslovakia in 1939 following German occupation and returned again as President briefly between 1946 and 1948 before the complete communist takeover.

Daladier, Edouard (1884–1970): French Radical Party politician who became Prime Minister as well as Minister of War in 1938 after the fall of the Popular Front government. He left office in May 1940 and was imprisoned by the Germans when France was occupied.

There are a number of explanations for Hitler's decision to back away from war. He was under strong pressure from his own generals and from party leaders to back down rather than risk a general war for which Germany was not yet prepared. Though Hitler's instinct was to see through the crisis with sheer willpower, he was deeply affected by the widespread evidence that the German public, like populations all over Europe, did not want war. As news of the crisis spread, according to one eyewitness, 'a wave of disappointment, indignation and panic spread throughout Germany . . . the fearful shock could be read plainly in people's faces' (Overy, 1998: 49). When no less a figure than Goering came to see him on the morning of 28 September counselling caution, Hitler capitulated. The following day Chamberlain, Daladier, Hitler and Mussolini met at Munich to work out a solution to the Sudeten question. The Soviet Union was not invited on the grounds that fascist leaders would never agree to sit with communists; in reality Chamberlain felt, almost certainly correctly, that Stalin would never voluntarily agree to the dismemberment of Czechoslovakia with whom the Soviet Union had a pact of mutual assistance. Hitler was granted the Sudetenland at Munich in return for vague promises of future good behaviour [**Doc. 8, p. 107**], but his demeanour throughout the conference betrayed his frustration and anger at being forced once again to work within a framework which had been dictated by the victor powers of 1918.

War was averted in 1938 because no one, not even Germany, was willing or able to risk it. The Munich pact was not an honourable agreement [**Doc. 9, p. 108**], for it left the Czechs at the mercy of great power diplomacy, just as they had been in 1919, but it did prevent Hitler from doing just what he wanted in eastern Europe. Yet given the framework within which British and French diplomacy was conducted, with a disintegrating world order in Europe, the Far East and the Mediterranean, and pressures at home generated by public hostility to war, economic vulnerability and military unpreparedness, the Munich Agreement represented a realistic assessment of the balance between western interests and western capabilities. Though with hindsight we might conclude that something vital had been at stake in the Czech crisis, it was not immediately obvious in 1938, when Chamberlain was universally hailed as the saviour of peace. It seemed to some that an element of stability might now be restored to European affairs. The Munich pact laid down the limited terms which Britain would accept for treaty revision in Europe, and it gave the appearance that Hitler had been compelled, like Beneš, to accept Britain and France as final arbiters in Europe. This fact above all persuaded Chamberlain that the prospect of a general settlement was not yet beyond his grasp. The Agreement opened up the prospect of settling those economic and colonial issues which were thought to be the last stumbling blocks to agreement.

3

Economic and Imperial Rivalry

N o single factor was more important in explaining the breakdown of the diplomatic system in the 1930s than the world economic crisis. What began as a slow fall in the business cycle in 1929 quickly accelerated into a recession of such intensity that unemployment rose to between one-fifth and one-third of the industrial workforce in the advanced economies. The system of world trade and finance, already in difficulties during the 1920s because of war debts and a weak pound, collapsed. The value of trade fell 70 per cent between 1929 and 1932. In 1931 Austria, and then Germany, came to the brink of national bankruptcy. Only a timely moratorium on all debts, initiated by the United States, prevented the world credit system from seizing up altogether.

The effects of the recession were immediate and far-reaching. The prices of foodstuffs and raw materials collapsed, leaving the poorer primary-producing countries and European and American farmers faced with a sharp fall in income, which in turn reduced demand for manufactured goods and pushed up unemployment and bankruptcies. In response, governments sought ways of protecting their own producers and preserving trade at the expense of other countries. A deeply protectionist mood took root everywhere. American tariffs were sharply increased in 1930. France manipulated its currency to remain competitive abroad. Most alarming of all, Britain, the financial centre of the world market, finally abandoned the commitment to free trade and the gold standard and established a system of protection known as **Imperial Preference**, which was established at the Ottawa Imperial conference in 1932. The investment that had flowed from London and Paris to oil the wheels of the world economy, already slowly declining during the 1920s, was reduced to a trickle after 1929, leaving smaller and weaker economies faced with serious currency and payments problems. This engendered a growing mood of resentment and disillusionment with the capitalist system in general, and with the more powerful trading economies in particular (Kindleberger, 1973; Boyce, 1989).

Imperial Preference: Protective trade system agreed by Britain and the Dominions at the Ottawa Imperial Conference in 1932. Britain agreed to give preference to imperial imports of food and raw materials and the Dominions agreed to take more British industrial goods.

Autarky: A policy of economic self-sufficiency, made at the expense of international trade.

Such resentment was expressed in the spread of ideas of self-sufficiency, or **autarky**. In order to avoid remaining at the mercy of fluctuations in the world economy, it was argued that national economies should become as independent as possible of the world system, providing as much of their food and industrial requirements as they could with domestically produced substitutes. This view was popular in the fascist states, where economic independence was seen as desirable on nationalist grounds, and was first practised with mixed success in Mussolini's Italy. It was taken up as a major political objective after 1933 by the Hitler government, which blamed Germany's difficulties on foreign capitalists and bankers. Though it proved neither possible nor desirable to cut Germany off completely from the world economy, German trade remained at a low level and was closely controlled by the state, while foreign loans were excluded as far as possible. But if autarky was regarded in ideological terms, as an expression of national economic virility, it was to some extent forced upon Italy and Germany by economic circumstances. Mussolini argued that the world was divided up into 'plutocratic' and 'proletarian' nations. Britain, France and the United States were very wealthy economies with vast material resources at their disposal. Germany, Italy and Japan were poor in natural resources, lacked great international wealth and were always in danger of being denied markets and raw materials by the 'plutocracies'.

'Have-not' nations: Major states that lacked a large territorial empire or adequate access to raw materials or markets. These contrasted with the 'have' states of Britain, France and the United States.

The distinction between 'have' and **'have-not' nations**, whatever its intellectual drawbacks, was a widely discussed and popular idea in the 1930s, and not only in Italy and Germany. It had its origins well before 1914 in arguments about the purpose of empire. Now, in the light of the economic slump, the idea was revived that there existed a demonstrable relationship between economic success and colonies, notwithstanding the awkward evidence that the most successful economy, the United States, was not an imperial power in any formal sense at all. The more Britain and France were forced to fall back on their empires for economic revival in the 1930s, the more forcefully the 'have-not' powers asserted their own right to empire. The world economic crisis thus had the effect of sharpening conflicts over markets and raw materials, undermining economic co-operation, and arousing once again dreams of imperial conquest.

Mandates: Colonies and territories taken under League control from Germany and Turkey in 1919. They were allocated as 'mandates' to Britain, France and Japan, who were responsible for their administration though they were not formally part of their empires. In practice they were treated like colonial territories except for Iraq, which was granted its full independence in 1932.

THE IMPERIAL POWERS

Imperial expansion did not disappear in 1918. When Britain and France took over German colonies and Turkish territories as **mandates** held on trust for the League of Nations, their empires reached their fullest extents. To the Far East and Africa were added territories throughout the Middle East. Britain's empire embraced 23.9 per cent of the land area of the globe; French territories comprised a further 9.3 per cent (Betts, 1991: 5). It is important to realize the extent and size of British and French imperial interests, and the persistence with which they were upheld, if sense is to be made of western diplomacy in the years before the outbreak of war [Map 1, p. xxix].

Empire was regarded by both powers as a vital interest. If at times it appeared a liability, no government (right or left) during the interwar years was prepared to consider abandoning the imperial heritage or seriously questioned why Britain and France should have an empire at all. The mere possession of empire became justification enough. Without the empire Chamberlain thought Britain would be 'a fourth-rate power' (Tamchina, 1972: 100). Empire was the source of Britain's greatness, the vehicle for the spread of French culture. French colonialists conjured up the vision of a new Mediterranean empire 'to extend the space occupied by our civilisation' (Andrew and Kanya-Forstner, 1981: 238) and planned a great imperial rail-way from Paris across the Sahara desert to the Congo. In 1931 Paris hosted an International Colonial Exposition that gave physical expression to the imperial ideal.

In 1924 London had already laid on a magnificent Empire Exhibition at the newly built Wembley arena. Here territories old and new were repres-ented – Tanganyika, South-West Africa and Palestine acquired in 1919, side by side with the old settler territories, Canada, Australia, New Zealand. The British now fully controlled the 'all-red route' from Britain to Asia. Gibraltar, Malta, Cyprus, Suez, Aden, Somaliland were all stepping stones to India, the centre-piece of the British Empire. That India should be defended was taken for granted. 'There will be no "lost dominion",' said **Lord Birkenhead**, 'until the moment – if ever it comes – when the whole British Empire with all that it means for civilisation, is splintered into doom' (Porter, 1996: 300). British prestige and world influence were so closely bound up with empire that there was never any serious doubt that Britain would fight to retain it. 'We have got most of the world already, or the best parts of it,' wrote Britain's First Sea Lord in 1934, 'and we only want to keep what we have got and prevent others from taking it away from us' (Pratt, 1975: 3).

Above all, empire was assumed in an altogether uncritical way to be a source of economic advantage. On this ground the public at large could be persuaded that imperialism was in their interest as well, and did not stem purely from a desire for territorial aggrandizement and world power. In the aftermath of the 1929 slump, as British and French trade declined, the empires did indeed become relatively more important. France's investment in its empire rose from 9 per cent of her total overseas investment in 1914 to 45 per cent by 1940. Trade with the empire increased from 12 per cent of all

Birkenhead, Earl of (1872–1930): The Con-servative politician and lawyer F.E. Smith, who became Lord Chancellor in 1919 when he was ennobled, and between 1924 and 1928 was Secretary of State for India.

French trade in 1929 to almost a third by 1936. The empire was a vital source of French supplies of rice, rubber, cocoa, coffee and valuable minerals (Andrew and Kanya-Forstner, 1981). In Britain the economic connection became even more important. Exports to the empire rose from one-third to almost half of all British exports between 1910 and 1938. The amount of overseas investment from Britain going to the empire increased to 59 per cent of the total by 1930 against only 7.9 per cent invested in Europe (Catterall and Morris, 1993: 13). Britain's Colonial Secretary talked in 1925 of Britain's tropical empire whose economic possibilities 'are perhaps greater than those available to us anywhere else in the world . . . immense territories, with immense natural resources' (Porter, 1996: 278).

Sentiments such as these served to reinforce the view abroad that British economic strength rested on its empire rather than through closer economic ties with Europe. Imperial protection was regarded by many as a natural expression of this special relationship in a world where free trade could no longer be practised with profit. Empire was presented to the electorate not as a moral mission but as a source of strength and advantage over other powers. Economic stability, and hence political stability, was said to hinge on empire. This in turn made the defence of empire, and fears for its safety, a central part of British foreign policy in the 1930s and a major factor in the pursuit first of appeasement, then of war.

In fact the advantage of empire was largely a delusion. Far from being a source of strength it was a growing liability, seriously undermining the capacity of both Britain and France to pursue their foreign policy goals, or to contain the aggressor powers. Imperialism strained relations between Britain and France at every turn, but especially in the Middle East, in Syria and Lebanon. The empires themselves were a constant source of friction and violence, with the spread of nationalism from Europe to the colonial world and the growth of an educated native political class. For all the talk of unity, the British Empire was in the slow throes of disintegration. Ireland was lost in 1922 with the signing of the Anglo-Irish Agreement and the creation of the Irish Free State in the south of the island. The Dominions were granted full autonomy in 1926. Years of nationalist struggle in India produced the Government of India Act in 1935 which paved the way for greater self-government. In 1936 the Anglo-Egyptian Treaty was signed which provided for greater parity between the two states and for joint control of the Suez Canal. South Africa, now dominated by those very same Boers that Britain had defeated in 1902, was increasingly unsympathetic, while the other white dominions, although sensitive to British needs, were far from firm in their support of the mother country. During the Czech crisis in 1938 the Dominions counselled any action that would avoid the risk of war. The Canadian Prime Minister, **Mackenzie King**, thought this was 'the one means of saving the Empire'.

King, Mackenzie (1874–1950): Canadian Liberal politician who was Prime Minister three times, the third time from 1935 to 1948 when he played an important part in persuading Canadian opinion to follow Britain into war in 1939 and offering extensive financial and material aid during the war.

Lord Zetland, Secretary of State for India, warned that war in 1938 would unleash nationalist revolt in Asia and the Middle East (Boyce, 1989: 282; Catterall and Morris, 1993: 114).

In many of the remaining parts of the dependent empire Britain was compelled to use force to prevent the erosion of its power. By 1939 a large part of Britain's military forces was on station in the Middle East. Political unrest was forcibly suppressed in Iraq, Egypt, Palestine and India. Nor was the French Empire any more secure despite French ambitions to create a single political and economic bloc by 'assimilating' colonies with the mother-country. Civil war in the Middle East, Arab revolt in North Africa, and communist agitation in Indo-China (where by 1932 there were 10,000 political prisoners) underlined the fragility of the empire. French colonial methods were harsh and inflexible. Throughout the empire high taxes, collective fines on villages, forced labour and summary execution were the price of French control. Its evidence in Syria proved too much even for the British, who forced the French to grant concessions. French colonialists were by and large still imbued with what the French **Marshal Lyautey** called 'the belief in inferior races whose destiny is to be exploited' (Andrew and Kanya-Forstner, 1981: 245).

The British and French Empires failed to excite popular enthusiasm at home, except among those upper- and middle-class groups whose livelihood and influence were dependent on colonies, and among the soldiers and politicians for whom empire had a visionary, sentimental appeal. The gains from imperial trade were offset by considerable liabilities. Protection was, in the long run, of more benefit to the Dominions than to Britain (Drummond, 1974). India consumed more British resources than it returned. The military and administrative costs of empire were a constant source of concern to governments which, in more sober mood, became increasingly reluctant to bear the burden of empire. This was the great paradox of Franco-British strategy between the wars. Those same empires that were perceived to make Britain and France into world-class powers, the foundation of their security and strength abroad, were in practice a source of mounting insecurity and crisis. To defend them adequately required so great an expenditure of resources as to threaten the very stability the empires were supposed to provide. Yet failure to defend them was perceived as an end to British and French world power, which neither was prepared to accept.

Lyautey, Marshal Hubert (1854–1934): French general who spent most of his army career in the colonies. He became the first Resident-General in French Morocco from 1912 to 1925.

THE 'HAVE-NOT' POWERS

The hard realities of imperialism did nothing to deflect the 'have-not' powers from their appetite for empires of their own. On the contrary, the weaknesses of the French and British Empires were regarded as evidence that they were declining forces in world affairs, fit for overthrow by younger, more vigorous nations. Looking at the example set by Britain and France, the 'have-nots' assumed that territorial expansion and foreign rule were invariable features of the international system. As one empire fell, others arose to take its place. These ambitions were dressed up in the language of economic grievances and their just redress. In all three 'have-not' powers, Germany, Italy and Japan, there existed circles which assumed that their country's long-term economic interests, indeed the very survival of their peoples, depended on the acquisition of large areas of conquered territory to be used as a source of materials and cheap labour and for the resettlement of surplus people from the home country. That much of this was in fact an illusion, since economic growth depended on a great many other variables, was never seriously considered. In the end the quest for empire developed a momentum of its own, independent of economic ambition, a product of hazy notions of racial destiny and delusions of imperial grandeur borrowed from an earlier age.

There was, of course, an element of truth in such arguments. The geopolitical circumstances of the Axis powers in the interwar years did affect their economic performance and prospects for social stability. When compared with the richer states, Italy was short of almost all major industrial raw materials. So, too, was Japan until its conquest of northern China. Germany had lost a large part of its coal and iron deposits through the Versailles Settlement, and lacked secure sources of oil. Oil was particularly important as a vital strategic material for aircraft, ships and the new mechanized armies. Although all three powers could be supplied with oil through normal trading channels, the sources of supply were easy for an enemy to intercept, and the arrangements for buying and shipping the oil difficult to operate. German and Italian supplies of iron ore were vulnerable on the same count. In the deteriorating conditions of world trade in the 1930s such fears seemed real enough.

Access to world markets and sources of capital was also fraught with difficulties. Japan found itself progressively excluded from Asian and African markets by British and French protective measures aimed largely at Japanese goods. German trade and investment were replaced in central Europe and the Balkans by those of Britain and France after 1919. Other forms of discrimination were introduced. Italian emigration to the United States was restricted after the First World War; Japanese emigration to Australia and America was closed off by the 1930s. The populations of both countries continued to grow at a high rate, a fact that exacerbated the impact of unemployment and low incomes in the years of world recession. No doubt Japan, Germany and Italy were inclined to grumble more than was necessary. Their economies experienced relatively high rates of growth during the 1920s. Nor were the protectionist measures taken by the western powers simply the product of deliberate malice, but of perceived economic self-interest (and to some extent as a retaliation against protectionism in the 'have-not' nations themselves). What mattered was that the slowing down in economic and trade growth and the spread of protectionism were regarded by political forces in the three countries as a deliberate attempt to restrict and inhibit the natural expansion of the new economies.

It was thus the *political* hostility that economic rivalry produced which mattered. Expression was given to this hostility not only through the ambitions of the dictators themselves, but also through the economic and imperial demands of political parties – the fascists in Italy, the National Socialists in Germany, nationalist and military associations in Japan – and through the expansionist demands of the armed forces. The economic complaints became subsumed in less rational arguments about the necessity for military and territorial expansion. While it would be wrong to maintain that there existed a coherent and pre-planned timetable for war, it is impossible to ignore the powerful evidence that war and conquest became major ambitions in all three states during the 1930s. Pushed on by economic circumstances and the pressure of political nationalism at home, all three powers sought to redress the balance of world affairs in their own favour.

Japanese expansion did not begin with the invasion of Manchuria, but with the occupation of Korea in 1894. During the First World War and the 1920s piecemeal expansion continued. Arguably in the Japanese case the pressure to go further than this and occupy Manchuria was based on a fear of Russia and China and the search for an effective buffer state, as Japanese leaders claimed. But this is to ignore the steady pressure to extend Japanese power throughout the western Pacific seaboard, and the continued encroachment on Chinese sovereignty from Manchuria, once it had been occupied. Nor does it adequately explain the colonial character of Japanese rule in Korea and Manchuria, whose economies and labour force were made to conform with Japanese requirements on unfavourable terms. Nevertheless, Japanese civilian politicians, though committed to the extension of Japanese power, were more opportunistic and cautious in their diplomacy than their military colleagues. Not until the army revolt of 1936 did pressure grow at home to extend Japanese influence throughout eastern Asia. The failure of the other major Pacific powers to restrain Japan encouraged greater risk-taking. In 1938 Japan sought to give its expansion more coherence by establishing an Asian 'New Order' based upon Japanese military and economic hegemony in northern and eastern China, and cultural and diplomatic pressure elsewhere [**Doc. 10, p. 109**]. This laid the foundation for the so-called '**Co-Prosperity Sphere**' set up during the war, which stretched from Manchuria in the north to Burma and the Dutch East Indies in the south. At no point in this expansion were Japanese leaders prepared to abandon any of

Co-Prosperity Sphere: Sphere of influence set up by Japan in Asia in the late 1930s. The idea was to demonstrate to other Asian states that they would all benefit from the Japanese domination of the region through building an integrated economic bloc, but the system was designed chiefly to benefit Japan.

their conquests. They ignored the Brussels Conference called in November 1937 by Roosevelt to discuss the future of China, and actively sought to extend their influence into the European colonial territories in the Far East (Jones, 1954; Louis, 1971). In 1937 a great programme of autarky was announced, designed in five years to double Japan's domestic output of iron and steel, increase machine-tool output fourfold, and oil output by a factor of fifteen, using new techniques of synthetic oil production (Barnhart, 1981).

Italian expansion too was carried out within areas of historic Italian concern: North and East Africa, the Dalmatian coast, and the islands of the Mediterranean. Mussolini blended together old-fashioned colonialism and fascist ideology. 'Fascism', it has been said, 'lived on dreams of future prosperity' (Kindleberger, 1973: 107). Empire was pursued in order to make the Italian people wealthy, but it was also to give them a sense of racial superiority. Only through recreating the old Roman Empire in the Mediterranean and Near East, argued Mussolini, could fascism provide full expression for the vigorous leadership and the harsh, heroic values of the movement. Brought up on propaganda and rhetoric about the glories of Mussolini's new Italy, Italians needed somewhere to rule [**Doc. 11, p. 110**]. Mussolini actively built up the Italian armed forces to a point where he believed Italy was strong enough to begin its civilizing mission. As opportunities presented themselves, this crude vision of empire was gradually adopted as Italian national policy. Ethiopia was the corner-stone of this new imperialism. Fascist writers argued that it was rich in raw materials and would become the industrial heartland of Africa. Vast areas for the settlement of Italian emigrants were seized from Ethiopian owners. Libya was to be developed in the same way. In all the Italian conquests colonial government was introduced. Racial laws were enacted in 1937 to prevent miscegenation in the East African colonies. Colonial governors were instructed not to see the colonies as areas being slowly nursed to self-government, but as areas ripe only for domination by a superior culture (Mack Smith, 1976).

Sooner or later, Mussolini realized, he would have to confront Britain and France in both Africa and the Mediterranean. Because neither power had opposed the conquest of Ethiopia by force, and had not prevented Italy's intervention in Spain, Mussolini came to assume that it was only a matter of time before he could replace them as the major power in the region. When Chamberlain visited Rome in January 1939 Mussolini told his Foreign Minister: 'These men are not made of the same stuff as the Francis Drakes and the other magnificent adventurers who created the [British] Empire' (Muggeridge, 1947: 9–10). Four months later he sent Italian troops to occupy Albania, threatening Yugoslavia to the north and Greece to the south, but also threatening Britain's vital interests in the Middle East. Italy now had, according to its ambassador in London, **Dino Grandi**, 'complete dominion

Grandi, Dino (1895– 1988): Italian fascist politician who became Foreign Minister from 1929 to 1932 and then Ambassador to London between 1932 and 1939. He played an important part in forcing Mussolini from office in the summer of 1943 but then fled to Spain to avoid a death sentence from the new fascist regime.

over the eastern Mediterranean' (Mack Smith, 1976: 154). There was a good deal of wishful thinking in Italian policy, but much of Italian military planning during the years from 1936 onwards was directed at building up the military and naval means to strike at British and French areas of influence or control. Much of the recent historical writing on Mussolini's imperialism has emphasized its serious intent and the extent to which fascism was driven by the vision of a 'restored' Italian hegemony throughout the Mediterranean basin. Though at times Mussolini may have seen the tactical advantage of talking to the British or the French, from the Ethiopian War the principal element in Italian foreign policy was the 'Axis' with Germany which might make possible an enlarged Italian Empire on the back of German support. This meant, in the end, risking major war. But war, Mussolini once declared, was 'the normal condition of peoples and the logical aim of any dictatorship' (Mack Smith, 1976: 202).

German ambitions differed in a number of important respects from those of Italy and Japan. The latter powers were concerned chiefly with the establishment of a geographically defined hegemony, the one in the Mediterranean basin, the other in east Asia. Under Hitler, Germany sought world power. Before 1914, German expansionists had looked mainly to central and eastern Europe as a 'natural' area of German influence. Overseas colonies were never as important as they were to the western powers, though many Germans would have liked to have them back after Versailles. But Hitler's vision of empire transcended the traditional aims of German foreign policy. It was a vision little more coherent and consistent than that of Italy and Japan. Though it was shared widely with other leaders of the party, it derived its strength and scope from Hitler alone. The concept of empire was central to his world view. It grew out of Hitler's ideas on the historical necessity of struggle between different races and cultures, and his belief that alone among nations only Germans and Jews seriously contested for world-historical power. Hence if Germany were to fulfil its historic mission then the major western powers and the Soviet Union, all of which Hitler came to regard as degenerate and corrupted by the Jews, had to be pushed aside and world Jewry destroyed in the process. Historians have recently argued that Hitler's vision extended as far as a conflict with the United States, whose racial heterogeneity Hitler despised, and whose material culture challenged his conception of a revitalized European civilization.

These were not mere dreams, though they may have seemed so when Hitler wrote them down in the 1920s. Once in power they formed the loose framework for the conduct of foreign policy and domestic affairs. Specific plans were gradually unfolded as Hitler consolidated his political position at home. Many Germans, and not just the party faithful, welcomed the remilitarization of Germany. They supported too the efforts to revise the Versailles

Mitteleuropa: The area of central Europe including Germany, Austria, Hungary and Poland. It was usually regarded as a potential economic bloc and a sphere for German influence, rather than an area of political influence implied by the term *Lebensraum*.

Pan-Germanism: The concept of uniting all ethnic Germans in a single political unit. There were Pan-German movements in pre-1914 Germany and Austria which influenced Hitler's later Pan-German aspirations in the 1930s.

Lebensraum: Term commonly used in Germany in the 1920s and 1930s to describe that amount of territory thought to be necessary to allow a nation to feed and provision itself to a reasonable standard. The search for 'living space' became the excuse for programmes of territorial expansion. In Italy the concept was called *il spazio vitale*.

Thirty-Years' War: European-wide conflict in Europe between 1618 and 1648 which was characterized by extreme levels of violence against the civilian population.

Speer, Albert (1905–81): German architect who was commissioned by Hitler to help rebuild Germany's largest cities in the 1930s. He was appointed Armaments Minister in February 1942, and was later tried at Nuremberg, where he was sentenced to twenty years.

Treaty. But for Hitler this was a mere beginning, while the foundations were laid for massive warfare in the future and the German people were psychologically prepared for the experience of total war. German empire was to be acquired in two complementary stages [**Doc. 12, p. 111**]. In the first stage Germany was to establish without general war the old idea of *Mitteleuropa*, a central and eastern European area dominated by Germany which could be used to provide the material resources (coal, iron ore, labour, oil) necessary for the prosecution of the next stage.

This initial stage called for a **Pan-German** solution – union with Austria, the incorporation of the German-speaking areas in Czechoslovakia and Poland – together with the economic and political subordination of the rump Czech and Polish states, Hungary and the remaining states of south-east Europe. By 1937 Hitler was ready to embark on this first wave. The timing and character of the construction of *Mitteleuropa* depended on diplomatic opportunity and on the pace of German military preparations. But there is no doubt that Hitler had both a foreign policy conception and a rough timetable for its achievement. Once German domination of central and eastern Europe was an accomplished fact, Germany would be in a position to develop the industrial and military resources as a springboard for the second stage of German expansion, the winning of an empire in the east.

The conquest of **Lebensraum**, or 'living space', in the east was a consistent feature of Hitler's thinking throughout the 1920s and 1930s. He believed that domination of the Eurasian heartland, what some geopoliticians regarded as the central core of any world system, would turn Germany into a global imperial power, dominating both Europe and Asia. He never laid down any clear plan for empire-building, but he hinted to his entourage on a number of occasions in 1936 and 1937 that a second great conflict, equal in intensity and violence to the rigours of the **Thirty Years' War**, would be unavoidable by the middle years of the 1940s. He told his pet architect, **Albert Speer**, to prepare the gigantic 'victory' buildings in Berlin for the early 1950s. He never disguised the fact that war was something that he expected Germany to fight at some time. In August 1936 he drafted a memorandum on strategy – the only major document Hitler wrote on foreign policy throughout the period of the Third Reich – which described the current international order in terms of one of the great transitional stages of world history, similar in its impact to the fall of the Roman Empire 1,500 years before. The struggle was not only for Germany's own birthright, but was also a contest between Bolshevism and its Jewish allies and the forces of European 'culture' represented and defended by Germany. The conquest of Eurasia was for Hitler not simply a product of economic or geopolitical necessity: its rationale lay ultimately in the ageless struggle between civilization and barbarism, culture and primitiveness, now expressed respectively by National Socialism and Bolshevism.

Was all this mere fantasy conjured up in the days of Hitler's political adolescence, or hollow rhetoric used to stir up domestic enthusiasm for the regime? Neither seems likely. Despite their fantastic and irrational character, there can be little doubt that Hitler's convictions were held with an almost messianic intensity, and that he meant, if he could, to put them into practice. This was by no means a straightforward process. Until the mid-1930s German foreign policy was strongly influenced still by traditional diplomatic circles. Within the Nazi Party itself there were a great many conflicting strands; Hitler himself was never entirely consistent in his views on international issues. It was only by 1938, when the conservative allies of the Nazi movement were almost all removed from office and replaced by Nazi politicians, that Hitler came to dominate the formation of foreign policy and military strategy. As Hitler's political position solidified so the ability or willingness of individuals to restrain Hitler diminished. The choice of war and grandiose imperialism was Hitler's, and it flourished only because of the nature of the dictatorship which had developed by the late 1930s. Hitler's vision became, willy-nilly, the vision for Germany as a whole. 'All the time,' Goering told business leaders in the autumn of 1938, 'my thoughts are circling round one thing. When will war come? Shall we win? What can we do?' (Overy, 1984: 78).

There was, nevertheless, as in France and Britain, a considerable gap between dream and reality for all three 'have-not' powers. Disagreement existed among the ruling élites over the conduct of foreign policy, particularly in Japan where some civilian ministers thought the risk of confronting Britain and the United States too high. In Italy imperialism was compromised by incompetence and corruption, and by the evident reluctance of the Italian people to assume the imperial role assigned to them by Mussolini. Few colonists could be found to take up the offer of land in Libya and Ethiopia, and those who did found themselves the victims of corrupt regional officials. The Italian military elite were also divided over the prospect of war, a fact to which Mussolini remained largely impervious. While some willingly embraced the detailed planning for a large new fleet to challenge British naval power in the Mediterranean, or drew up ambitious plans for the occupation of Egypt and Sudan in long cross-desert campaigns, others, and in particular Marshal Pietro Badolgio, the army Chief-of-Staff, were more cautious about Italy taking on more than it could easily accommodate. Even in Germany the conduct of foreign policy was conditioned at first by a necessary circumspection. German soldiers who entered the Rhineland in March 1936 had orders not to shoot if opposed by French or British troops. Yet with the success of each initiative, confidence grew in all three countries about the prospects for further expansion, narrowing down policy choices more rigidly in favour of war. Gradually foreign policy moved from the diplomacy of opportunity to the diplomacy of intention.

THE FAILURE OF 'ECONOMIC APPEASEMENT'

Much of the economic argument of the 'have-not' powers was understood in the west. The American Secretary of State thought that the rise of political nationalism was the 'characteristic expression of great people in revolt against the limitations placed upon their national prosperity by their poverty in natural resources'. Restoration of free trade and international prosperity would reduce the threat of war: 'discontent will fade and dictators will not have to brandish the sword and appeal to patriotism to stay in power' (Roberts, 1992: 89). Chamberlain shared this commercial view of world affairs: 'Might not a great improvement in Germany's economic situation result in her becoming quieter and less interested in political adventures?' he asked Halifax (Pratt, 1975: 138). There was an underlying assumption that Germany and Japan did have real economic claims which had to be respected, and that economic concessions in these areas would go far to eliminating the evident sense of grievance that both powers harboured towards the west.

This was the origin of economic appeasement. Beginning in 1936 the western powers sought to find terms on which the 'have-not' powers could be brought back fully into the world economy as a prelude to a general, and peaceful, settlement of outstanding political differences [Doc. 13, p. 112]. The real barrier to agreement was protection and exchange control, which blocked up the arteries of world trade and undermined prospects for a return to the more stable world economy of the 1920s. With Japan no satisfactory agreement could be reached, but preliminary agreements were reached in 1934 between Britain and Germany on trade and payments. British investors kept open credit lines to Germany which were worth £60 million by the outbreak of war in 1939. British traders provided valuable raw materials for German rearmament. Some rearrangement of eastern European trade was achieved in 1938. An agreement on coal exports was reached in January 1939. Britain also held out the prospect of a return of some German colonies as a sign of goodwill, to be accompanied by a substantial loan to Germany to ease what were assumed to be substantial trade and capital difficulties there. It was hoped that the promise of economic redress would persuade the more moderate elements in the German government to bring influence to bear on Hitler to take a more reasonable course and end the policy of autarky (Wendt, 1971).

In practice economic appeasement was no more successful than diplomacy in accommodating Germany and Japan within the western system. There were a number of reasons for this. First of all the western powers were unable to agree among themselves about economic reconstruction. The

World Economic Conference which met in London in June 1933 broke up in a matter of days on fundamental differences between America, Britain and France (Clavin, 1996). The stabilization of the international currency system in 1936 was the only major agreement between them. In 1938 the van Zeeland report drawn up by a League of Nations committee called for full international economic co-operation, but it was not acted upon. Britain was reluctant to make major concessions on imperial protection, which was the price America wanted for fuller economic co-operation. The brief economic recession in 1938 revived fears of another collapse like that of 1929 and temporarily pushed the powers back towards policies of economic nationalism. Most important of all, Italy, Germany and Japan were distrustful of western motives. Goering thought that more German exports would only serve to bolster western rearmament at Germany's expense. Far from being the 'moderate' that the west hoped, Goering was at the head of those groups in Germany transforming the economy to large-scale war preparations. The real moderates around **Schacht** were largely without political influence inside Germany. Nor were economic conditions there as poor as Britain thought; or at least not poor enough to throw Germany into the arms of its richer neighbours.

> **Schacht, Hjalmar** (1877–1970): German banker who was appointed Minister of Economics in Hitler's government in 1934 and in 1935 Plenipotentiary for War Economy. He helped to supply the finance for German rearmament, but he fell out with Hitler in 1937 and resigned.

Though Chamberlain hoped that economic appeasement would produce diplomatic dividends, and did so right up until the outbreak of war and even beyond, he also argued that Britain should use its considerable economic power as a weapon to contain the aggressor states: 'The idea was that we should use our financial strength and resources for political purposes' (Newman, 1976: 42). The outcome was a sharp acceleration in economic rivalry from the mid-1930s onwards, particularly in the Balkans and Middle East, in Latin America and in China, which occurred simultaneously with continued efforts at economic conciliation.

The situation in the Balkans and central Europe demonstrated this ambiguity. The region had long been regarded in the west as an area where Germany might pursue legitimate trading interests. During the German economic recovery after 1933 trade in the area was slowly built up on the basis of special treaties and bilateral payments agreements. Eastern European states bought manufactured goods and arms from Germany in return for raw materials and food which they could not sell easily in the west. British and French influence, particularly in Poland, Czechoslovakia and Hungary, declined relative to that of Germany. By 1938 Germany provided an average of 29 per cent of the exports of the countries of eastern and south-eastern Europe, and 29 per cent of their imports. Britain and France provided only 13.5 per cent and 11.2 per cent of exports and imports between them. Britain's reaction was to welcome German initiatives to the extent that they stabilized the area (particularly against the Russian threat), but to deplore the

Munich Agreement: Protocol signed by Germany, Britain, France and Italy on the evening of 29 September 1938 granting self-determination under German control to the German inhabitants of the Czech state, most of them in the area known as the Sudetenland.

collapse of freer trade in the area at its own expense [**Doc. 14, p. 112**]. In the discussions leading up to Munich a rough agreement was worked out dividing eastern Europe into different spheres of economic influence. Britain and France, both of which had begun to withdraw economically from central Europe even before the **Munich Agreement**, conceded this area to Germany in return for an understanding that they should be able to continue their economic activity in the Balkans and Turkey (Kaiser, 1980).

It was here that Britain and France were determined, if they could, to limit German expansion. Both states hoped to use their economic strength to hold up German economic penetration southwards. Turkey was regarded as vital in this respect, and was granted a credit of £16 million in May 1938 to secure its support. Greece and Romania were likewise promised financial aid and the prospect of more exports to the west during 1939 as part of a general, though rather ineffectual, strategy of containment. Compared with the British promise to buy limited quantities of Romanian wheat and Greek tobacco, the German negotiators offered a much more comprehensive package of loans, export agreements and arms. A long-term Romanian-German Trade Treaty was signed in March 1939. Generous trade credits were extended to Yugoslavia and loans negotiated in the autumn of 1938 with Turkey and Bulgaria. During 1939 British and French capital was progressively excluded from eastern Europe. The smaller Balkan countries, though anxious for more help from the west, were drawn further into the German net.

Similar rivalry sprang up in China and Latin America. In both areas America's 'Open Door' policy was repudiated. Germany made agreements similar to those made in the Balkans with the countries of Latin America. Japan sought to exclude western influence from northern China altogether and to dictate the terms on which loans and goods could be sent to the south. In both areas the response of the United States, though couched in the language of economic appeasement, was less compromising than the western response in the Balkans. In China American aid helped to stabilize the Chinese currency, while American loans (despite the Neutrality Act) sustained Chinese resistance to Japan. In their approach to Germany American statesmen argued in favour of economic pressure through a comprehensive trade agreement programme which, it was claimed, was 'a ready forged weapon in hand to induce Germany to meet world trade and political settlement' (Mommsen and Kettenacker, 1983: 393). When Germany refused to respond on American terms, economic conflict was intensified.

Did this mean that the war was in the end caused by economic rivalry? It was widely held in left-wing circles in the 1930s that wars were caused by capitalism. There is little direct evidence to support this view now. Business people in all countries favoured peace and the maintenance of international stability as a key to expanding trade and profits. In Germany, Italy and Japan many of the leaders of heavy industry and export industries were distrustful of extreme nationalism and the growing role of the state in economic affairs. Contacts were established between American, French, British and German industrialists, notably in chemicals and iron and steel, to reach international agreements on trade and output. Discussions between German and British businessmen continued into the summer of 1939. Of course, economic competition survived and indeed was strengthened during the 1930s, but it was not itself the cause of war. Had the aggressor powers simply been concerned with trade and raw materials, then they might well have been satisfied with economic concessions from the west, as many appeasers advocated. But Hitler and Mussolini and the Japanese nationalists could not be bought off. To them economic conflict had a basic political cause in the unequal distribution of territory and political influence. They politicized economic rivalry and expressed it in terms of a quest for empire. Economic settlement would only be possible once the political conflict was resolved.

Even Chamberlain, who more than anyone remained convinced that the dictators could be bought off by promises of economic gain, lamented in 1938 that 'Politics in international affairs governs actions at the expense of economics, and often of reason' (Leith-Ross, 1968: 247). If the war had a capitalist character at all, it was far more the case for Britain and France, where it was believed in governing circles that the international political crisis was directly caused by economic difficulties, and that the major threat posed to western interests was to their trade and financial influence, which in turn brought into question economic stability and political security at home. But even in Britain and France this problem was expressed not in crude economic terms (which would have been less popular at home) but in terms of empire and ideology. The war was fought in the end as a contest for political power, the culmination of that long and unstable period of empire-building which had begun in the middle of the nineteenth century.

4

Armaments and Domestic Politics

The contest for imperial and economic power could only be met by a great increase in military strength. Cadogan might well have spoken for all the powers when he told Chamberlain that 're-armament is a vitally necessary first step' without which 'it is difficult to have or to pursue a foreign policy' (Newman, 1976: 58). The level of armed strength crucially determined the willingness of the powers to risk war, and eventually the timing of war itself. During the 1920s limited disarmament was adopted by the major powers, not on grounds of international morality alone, but because no immediate military threat appeared on the international horizon. A higher level of military preparedness – especially for Britain and France, still the most heavily armed powers in the 1920s – would have been an unnecessary expenditure of industrial and human effort. During the depression military spending continued to fall. The Disarmament Conference, in session at Geneva between 1932 and 1934, called for serious efforts at multilateral reduction of arms as a prelude to the dawn of a new age of peace and plenty. The conference was soon overtaken by events. Growing international instability provoked the onset of worldwide rearmament.

REARMAMENT

Rearmament was not confined to Germany and the western powers. Japan and Italy continued to arm throughout the depression years, and the Soviet Union under Stalin embarked in 1929 on a series of Five-Year Plans part of whose object was the massive militarization of the Soviet Union in the face of the supposed threat from international capitalism. A great many lesser powers, China, Czechoslovakia, Poland, Spain and Turkey, pursued the same course. The League of Nations calculated that world military expenditure increased from $3.5 thousand million in 1925 to $5 thousand million in

1934. This increase was fuelled partly by distrust of the willingness or the ability of the League to enforce collective security; and partly by the desire of emergent nations to build up their own armed forces as a sign of national maturity, a vanity that the major arms producers were only too ready to satisfy. Trade in armaments increased sharply during the 1930s, from $34 million in 1932 to $60 million in 1937.

The German military threat really developed too late to be the main cause of this early rearmament. Britain was more concerned with Japan and Italy until 1935. But once the German threat became clearer, it encouraged the onset of a specific arms race between the three western powers which took place against the general background of world rearmament. This was inevitable once Britain and France identified Germany as the major threat to peace. Germany was committed to large-scale rearmament, though directed not only against the west but also against the growing size of Soviet armed forces. Britain and France used what they knew of German war preparations as a rough yardstick for their own military expenditure and arms plans.

All three powers believed that the next war, if it came, would be a total war: a long war that required the mobilization of the nation's entire military and moral resources. This was to some extent a natural reaction to the war of 1914, which the powers had expected to be 'over by Christmas', but which had lasted instead for four years. German generals analysed the nature of *totaler Krieg*, '**total war**'; French strategists talked of *la guerre de longue durée*. British strategy, with its central emphasis on naval power and financial strength, was always more committed to tactics of attrition and blockade than to short and decisive land campaigns. For Hitler the idea of a total war fitted in with his dreams of racial struggles of titanic proportions, of the final reckoning between the powers.

There were also very practical reasons for expecting a total war. The military leaders of the 1930s had all been through the experience of the First World War. Though a growing body of opinion among younger officers favoured ideas of the quick, mobile campaign fought by small professional armies, the main weight of military thinking was still expressed in terms of the western front: the machine gun, the artillery barrage, and conscript armies of huge size. The French **Maginot Line**, a long system of fortifications which resembled a heavily armed concrete 'trench', was built along the whole French border with Germany, though it remained incomplete when war came in 1939. The German military in 1938–9 built similar fortifications, the 'Westwall', on their side of the frontier. In the Soviet Union the 'Stalin Line', built in the late 1930s protected the long and vulnerable Soviet frontier in the west. The First World War also demonstrated the increasing industrialization of warfare. The armed forces had to be supplied with huge quantities of advanced military equipment, which required a total mobilization of

Total War: Term usually associated with the German general Erich Ludendorff, who in 1919 described the First World War as a 'total war' because it had demanded the total commitment of the economic, social and moral resources of the nation. It also described a war in which civilians as well as soldiers were part of the war effort and a legitimate target of attack.

Maginot Line: A series of defensive fortifications along France's eastern border, begun at the inspiration of the Defence Minister, André Maginot, in 1929, but still incomplete a decade later.

industrial and labour resources at home. The threat of blockade by the western powers, which the German army blamed for its eventual capitulation in 1918, gave added impetus to ideas about mobilizing the home front in Germany. The German army planned in the 1930s a comprehensive system of total mobilization which they called **Wehrwirtschaft** – the defence economy. French and British soldiers shared much of this view. In any future war victory would go only to the countries that produced the most military equipment. Since the full mobilization of such resources took time, the war would be a long-drawn out affair, a test of endurance.

Wehrwirtschaft: Term used to describe an economy geared to defence purposes, with a high level of investment, heavy industrial output and extensive plans for the conversion of civilian to military production in the event of war.

Preparation for such a conflict was a problem of enormous complexity. The scale of rearmament was a question of intelligent guesswork, but guesswork nonetheless. The scale of military preparations and the timing of production plans depended not only on the domestic resources available, but upon intelligence of what other powers were planning to produce. Additionally, account had to be taken of the rapid changes in military technology. Over the course of the 1930s the quality and performance of major weapons, particularly aircraft, altered dramatically. Wood and canvas biplanes gave way to all-metal single-wing aircraft of much higher performance. Radio and radar transformed military communications. By 1939 jet aircraft, rockets, even nuclear weapons, were in the early stages of development. Another crucial variable was a proper estimate of the number and character of potential enemies. For some powers this was much easier to calculate than for others. Japan and Italy, whose foreign policy depended to a great extent on winning local advantage over powers which were otherwise much stronger, concentrated on naval rearmament and fighter-bomber aircraft sufficient to achieve local superiority. The four major powers, Britain, the Soviet Union Germany and France, had to he prepared for every contingency.

German rearmament had begun in a very limited way before 1933. In February 1933 Hitler announced, amid general approval from the heads of the armed forces, a long-term plan for German military build up. But the first priority was to restore the infrastructure of military life, the barracks, airfields, fortifications and installations, that Germany had been denied under the conditions of the Versailles Treaty. This also meant a vast training programme to catch up with the other powers in the number of trained men and officers. Up to 1937 over 50 per cent of all German aircraft produced were trainers. Much of the military expenditure undertaken before 1939 went on buildings rather than the production of weapons. At the same time the armed forces, and the army in particular, set about planning for the economic co-ordination of the nation's resources should war eventually break out, a policy they christened 'armament in depth' instead of 'armament in width'. A special Plenipotentiary for War Economy was appointed in 1935. Every part of Germany belonged to a 'defence area' with its own armaments and economic staff who organized the mobilization of local economic resources (Carroll, 1968).

The effect of all this basic preparation was to reduce the proportion of military spending that Germany could actually devote to weapons and equipment, though rearmament was pursued so conspicuously and with such energy that foreign observers came away with the impression that Germany possessed large-scale and well-equipped armed forces sooner than was actually the case. In fact by 1936 German rearmament had reached something of a crisis point. Though the armed forces were happy to go on expanding until Germany had been restored to what they saw as its rightful weight in European affairs, the civilian ministers, led by the Minister of Economics, Hjalmar Schacht, were unhappy about the escalating cost of rearmament in a country slowly dragging itself out of the worst depression in its history. Hitler, however, had no reservations. In September 1936 he appointed Goering to head a new **Four-Year Plan** which was to be the foundation of Germany's preparation for total war [**Doc. 15, p. 113**]. Between 1936 and 1938 Goering came to acquire responsibility for large areas of the German economy and, with his circle of officials and appointees, greatly increased state control over the economy in order to push rearmament on faster (Simpson, 1959). In 1938–9 rearmament expenditure rose by 70 per cent above the level of the previous two years. The armed forces began to draw back, partly from fear of the effects excessive rearmament would have on the German economy, partly from a growing uncertainty about what Hitler was really preparing for.

But by now it was too late. Hitler was committed at some point to a war of 'great proportions'. A large programme for the production of synthetic strategic materials was set in motion. Hitler activated a new naval building programme in January 1939 to give Germany a great battle fleet once again. He ordered a quintupling of air force strength, including a strategic bomber force, and laid the foundations for an army with a large mechanized core. The end date for these preparations was fixed for the mid-1940s, when Germany would be ready, if necessary, to fight other great powers – even including, it has been argued, the United States, which historians have come to see as the ultimate showdown for Hitler after achieving the domination of Europe. In 1938 and 1939 this process was far from complete. There were no firm military plans for campaigns either to east or west, nothing to compare with the **Schlieffen Plan** of 1914. In order to mask the longer time-scale of German preparations Hitler pursued a policy of putting as much as possible in the 'shop window' to give the impression that Germany was armed in greater depth than was in fact the case (Deist, 1981; Overy, 1994b).

French strategy was based on the same expectation of a great war. French military thinkers argued that given France's smaller population and likely

Four-Year Plan: Plan for economic and military preparation for war drawn up by Hitler in August 1936 and formally launched under the direction of Hermann Göring in October. It was strictly speaking the second Four-Year Plan, following the first Four-Year Plan launched in 1933 to overcome unemployment.

Schlieffen Plan: Not so much a plan, as a set of operational suggestions first proposed by the German army Chief-of-Staff, Alfred von Schlieffen in 1904 as an answer to German encirclement by France and Russia. The plan was based on the idea of a swift defeat of France, followed by a redeployment to face and defeat Russia. It failed in 1914, turning the war into a contest of attrition.

resource deficiencies in the early stages of any war, it was necessary to plan a war in two stages. The first stage should be purely defensive, preventing the enemy from reaching French soil. In the late 1920s, under the inspiration of André Maginot, Minister of Defence, a defensive line was begun incorporating the massive firepower of artillery and machine guns, which was designed to make France impenetrable. The second stage was the building up of an offensive striking power, including heavy bombers, so great that it could eventually break out from the defensive line and overwhelm the German army by sheer volume of military material. **Marshal Pétain** argued that France could eventually produce twelve times as much equipment as the Germans, because of the effects of blockade on the German economy and the superior financial strength of France in world markets (Young, 1974, 1978).

The strategy of the total use of economic resources was accepted by French civilian and military leaders alike. But as in Germany it was difficult to get agreement about the level or pace of rearmament. French decisions had to be taken against a background of deteriorating economic conditions and growing political conflict between right and left. By 1937 French aircraft production was only a third that of Britain, one-eighth that of Germany. Overall military expenditure stagnated: 14 billion francs in 1932, and only 15 billion francs in 1936. Even this effort met resistance in French political circles because of the threat it posed to domestic stability at a time when capital was flooding out of France to escape the policies of the left-wing Popular Front. This slow expansion was less damaging to French interests than it appeared, however, since France had been until the mid-1930s the foremost military power in Europe and was still left with an important foundation on which to build. By 1939 military expenditure had increased sixfold over 1936. In tank and aviation technology France was at least the equal of Germany. Though there was ground to make up, it would be wrong to exaggerate the degree to which France was materially unprepared at the outbreak of war (Frankenstein, 1982). The problem was not lack of military resources, but the use to which these resources were put on the battlefield.

There were strong similarities in British strategic planning, though the pace of British rearmament was faster. Britain, like France, placed great emphasis on the need for effective defence. But Britain also hoped to build up sufficient armed force to act as a deterrent to other powers, making offensive action unnecessary: 'The fear of force is the only remedy,' thought Chamberlain (Feiling, 1946: 252). It was this that held Britain back from making any firm continental commitment before 1939. Rearmament was geared to British strengths rather than weaknesses. Britain lacked a large continental army because it had very different strategic priorities from Germany and France. Instead Britain hoped to use its economic strength and the traditional strategy of blockade and attrition to contain Germany in the event of

Pétain, Marshal Phillipe (1856–1951): French general who oversaw the building of the Maginot defences, but retired from the army in the 1930s. In June 1940 he assumed the role of Head-of-State with his capital in the French town of Vichy. In 1945 he was arrested and sentenced to life imprisonment for political crimes.

war, while building up an active air defence at home to prevent bombing and invasion. Economic power was regarded in this respect as vital. Like the French, British leaders were convinced that great financial and commercial strength offset any lead Germany might enjoy in military material. It was, argued **Thomas Inskip**, Minister for the Co-ordination of Defence, an essential element in Britain's defensive power, 'one which can properly be regarded as a fourth arm of defence, alongside the three Defence Services, without which purely military effort would be of no avail' (Pratt, 1975: 102–3). Naval power was also a vital concern. It was only through naval rearmament that effective defence of the route to India and Britain's Far Eastern empire could be established. The navy was one of the key instruments in the pursuit of an effective blockade of potential enemy powers, particularly Germany. Economic warfare could also be conducted from the air, through bombing attacks on an enemy's industry and the morale of its workforce. For that purpose, but with variable enthusiasm, the government supported the Royal Air Force in its efforts to build up a bomber striking-force during the 1930s. The great advantage of strategic bombing, as it was called, was thought to lie in the fact that Britain could bring the war to the European mainland from British bases without the need to commit large armies to a continental campaign. Indeed, some air strategists hoped that bombing on its own, through the attrition of enemy economic capacity, might act decisively to bring the war to an end.

All of these were long-war strategies, requiring the careful husbanding of resources and considerable planning for economic mobilization. Serious consideration of these long-term questions began in 1935 with the influential Defence Requirements Committee, first set up in November 1933. In March 1936 its conclusions formed the basis of a four-year plan for rearmament. Priority went to air force and naval expenditure and funds were 'rationed' on this basis. Expenditure increased from £185 million in 1936 to £719 million in 1939. There were plenty of critics who argued that not enough was being spent, or that the government's priorities were the wrong ones, particularly in the army, which was frustrated in its efforts to get army armaments any sort of priority. Certainly Baldwin and Chamberlain hoped initially that rearmament could be undertaken on the basis of a limited commitment which would not strain British resources too greatly, nor threaten political stability. But in 1937, when Chamberlain became Prime Minister, caution was thrown to the winds. Chamberlain ordered a full inquiry into the scope and purpose of Britain's rearmament plans. Together with the military leadership, he decided that Britain should prepare for total mobilization. As in France, a great armament effort was scheduled for 1938–40.

The Treasury, with some reluctance, released ever greater funds to meet the services' demands. Air plans were hurriedly revised upwards. Construction

Inskip, Thomas (1876–1947): Conservative politician and lawyer who was appointed as Minister for the Co-ordination of Defence from 1936 to 1939, and then became Lord Chancellor from 1939 to 1941. His role in promoting British rearmament was widely condemned as too little, too late.

of the great naval base at Singapore was speeded up. Mobilization plans were drawn up for the total utilization of Britain's economic and manpower resources. A defensive skeleton was built up between 1936 and 1939 which was to be fleshed out once war had actually started. In late 1938 mobilization preparation began in earnest. More funds were made available for the army, which had fallen behind the other two services in levels of preparedness, and a great effort was made to provide a large and modern air defence system based around radar and the most advanced monoplane fighters. By 1939, though no earlier, Britain was more prepared for a large war than its critics or enemies supposed (Peden, 1979; Shay, 1977).

How did this arms race affect the diplomatic situation? The mere existence of armaments does not of itself cause war. Rearmament clearly demonstrated the willingness of all the major powers involved to consider war as a future possible course of action, but until 1939 none of the powers, Germany included, was in a position militarily to risk major war. Rearmament plans took much time to complete. German plans were geared towards a major war in the mid-1940s. Detailed military campaign planning had only just begun in Germany in 1939. When war broke out in September only three major industrial sectors even had a mobilization plan; three more were in preparation, but nine sectors had no plan at all, including the aircraft and motor industries. British and French preparations, on the other hand, were planned to peak in 1939–40, since they could not afford a sustained high level of rearmament without risking political and economic crisis. Chamberlain would have preferred this increase in military force to act primarily as a deterrent against further aggression, but there can be no doubt that British and French policy in 1939 was powerfully influenced by the mounting evidence that the west was temporarily in a position not simply to deter, were that possible, but also to fight. This involved a great risk for both powers. Indeed there have been many critics then and since, who argued that Britain and France should have armed far sooner and to a much greater extent, since this might have avoided the element of risk altogether. But this is to ignore the many pressures on both governments – and for that matter on Hitler too – which made a faster rate of rearmament difficult to achieve however pressing its necessity.

The wild card in all these calculations was the Soviet Union. For long historians ignored the scale and effects of the Soviet military build-up in the 1930s because it was assumed that the arms race was between Germany and the west. The opening up of Soviet archives has made it possible to reassess the Soviet achievement and to understand that German military expansion was aimed as much at anticipating growing Soviet strength as it was at the potential threat in western Europe. From very modest beginnings Soviet military spending increased by leaps and bounds in the 1930s: 1.8 billion

Table 4.1 Military expenditure of the major powers, 1932–9

	France		Britain		Germany		Soviet Union	
	A billion fr	B %	A £ million	B %	A billion RM	B %	A billion rbls	B %
1932	13.8	5.0	103.3	2.5	0.76	0.8	4.03	2.97
1933	13.4	5.2	107.6	3.0	1.2	1.9	4.30	3.04
1934	11.6	4.9	113.9	3.0	3.6	4.1	5.40	3.48
1935	12.8	5.8	137.0	2.0	5.4	6.0	8.20	5.52
1936	15.1	6.3	185.9	5.0	10.2	10.8	14.80	7.80
1937	21.5	7.1	256.3	7.0	10.9	11.7	17.48	8.23
1938	29.1	8.6	397.4	8.0	17.2	17.2	27.04	12.51
1939	93.6	23.0	719.0	22.0	38.0	30.0	40.88	17.46

A Total military expenditure at current prices.
B Expenditure as a percentage of national product.
Figures for financial year 1 April–31 March

Sources: Dilks (1981: 35, 303); Ovendale (1975: 297); Overy (1979: 113); Overy (2004: 453)

Table 4.2 Aircraft production of the major powers, 1933–40

	France	Britain	Germany	Soviet Union
1933	–	633	368	2,595
1934	–	740	1,968	2,595
1935	785	1,140	3,183	2,529
1936	890	1,877	5,112	3,770
1937	743	2,153	5,606	4,435
1938	1,382	2,827	5,235	5,467
1939	3,163	7,940	8,295	10,382
1940	2,113	15,049	10,247	10,565

Source: Overy (1980: 21, 150)

roubles in 1931, 40.8 billion by 1939. By the end of the decade the Soviet Union had more combat aircraft and tanks than any other power, and a conscript army of over 4 million. Soviet thinking was also based on the idea of total war and Soviet society was bombarded with patriotic and militaristic propaganda to prepare the population for mass mobilization. The heavy industry at the core of the Five-Year Plans of the 1930s was designed to be converted to a war footing in the event of a sudden attack. Stalin played a key part in driving along the pace of Soviet rearmament. He did not seek war but he could see in the deteriorating climate of the 1930s that the

only communist state in the world needed to be able to defend itself effectively. By the late 1930s plans were laid down for building what was called
a 'Big Ocean-Going Fleet' of fifteen battleships and forty-four other major
warships, all to be completed by 1947. The rapid emergence of a Soviet
superpower in the 1930s anticipated the later Cold War conflict. Hitler's
Germany was aware that a very large armed force now stood on the edge of
central Europe; Britain was anxious about Soviet ambitions in Asia and India;
Japan knew that any encroachment in Asia or the Pacific might give the
Soviet Union the excuse to intervene in the Far East. The rise of Soviet power
had to be incorporated into the thinking of the non-communist world alongside all the other external and domestic pressures it faced.

FINANCE, INDUSTRY AND LABOUR

The scale and speed of rearmament depended on the extent to which Britain,
Germany and France could cope with the constraints placed on their military
preparations through financial pressures, shortages of industrial capacity and
labour. These were the major determinants of the economic effort behind
rearmament. They assumed a special significance because the military plan-
ners in all three countries expected a future war to be won by the degree of
economic mobilization each could achieve.

Preparation for total war was very expensive. To find the necessary sums
in peace time invited a whole range of difficulties: a reduction in living standards, the prospect of inflation, excessive government borrowing (excessive,
that is, by the orthodox financial standards of the 1930s) and cut-backs in
social programmes. These risks seemed all the greater in a Europe slowly
recovering from the effects of the world recession. Governments were reluctant to risk fragile financial stability for the sake of large-scale armaments. In
Germany this produced a growing crisis by 1936. Rearmament of limited
scope had contributed to the rapid recovery of the German economy. In
1936 Hitler wanted to use this stronger economy to accelerate rearmament
well beyond the levels originally planned. Schacht and the orthodox bankers
and industrialists objected that Germany could not afford the cost, and
should concentrate instead on exports. Germany had experienced the damaging hyperinflation of 1923. Large expenditure on arms carried the risk of
inflation once again, and with it the possibility of political unrest. Hitler's
answer was to bring the economy more closely under state control and party
influence. The financial markets in Germany were strictly regulated. Government loans were floated to pay for rearmament and taxes kept at high levels.
The growth of the civilian sector was deliberately restricted. Consumption as

a percentage of national income declined from 71 per cent in 1928 to 59 per cent in 1938. The Minister of Finance, **Count Schwerin von Krosigk**, complained that the sums required to pay for rearmament would, by 1939, cripple the German economy. Historians now generally agree that the financial crisis did not materialize thanks to the close control of the capital and currency markets now exercised by the German state, but finance was not, it has been argued, the central issue. The problem rearmament posed for the German economy was one of the balance of payments. The difficulties faced in acquiring the materials to sustain military production may in the end have played an important part in the decision to seize those resources by force, though the evidence of a foreign policy driven by economic necessity remains ambiguous at best (Overy, 1987; Tooze, 2006).

A much better case can be made for the argument that the economic costs of rearmament threatened to provoke crisis in the western democracies. Fear of the damaging economic and political effects of big increases in government expenditure slowed down the pace of rearmament in both France and Britain. In 1936 and 1937 the Popular Front government in France placed a high priority on social welfare programmes and increased living standards, but also wanted to increase rearmament to meet the fascist threat. The inflationary impact on the currency undermined efforts to improve living standards and invited a crisis with labour as well. Though new sums for rearmament were raised they required an increase in government debt which threatened budgetary stability. When military expenditure was raised again in the spring of 1938 to even higher levels, **Georges Bonnet**, the Foreign Minister, painted an alarming picture of the consequences: 'if France should have to continue to arm at the present rate it would be necessary to regiment the entire population, placing the civilian population on soldiers' wages and soldiers' rations' (Adamthwaite, 1977: 27).

British politicians shared this fear of excessive financial burdens. Rearmament was tolerable, Inskip thought, only 'without making demands on our resources which would impair stability' (Newman, 1976: 21). Chamberlain was haunted 'with the sense that the burden of armaments might break our backs' (Newman, 1976: 58). Britain, too, was concerned to maintain political and economic stability by not sacrificing too readily either living standards or social expenditure. Nevertheless the pressure of international events after 1936 pushed the government towards increased military outlays. Research has shown that the conventional view of the Treasury and Bank of England resisting the financial demands of rearmament must be modified (Peden, 1979). The Treasury ensured that the money was spent as effectively as possible, and would release no funds without a good case for their necessity, but in the end no serious constraints were placed on rearmament by a shortage of finance. Rearmament was met by a combination of tax increases,

Krosigk, Schwerin von (1887–1977): German Finance Ministry official who was appointed Finance Minister in Germany in 1932 and kept the office until 1945. He was responsible for helping to finance German rearmament and the financial exploitation of Europe but avoided indictment as a major war criminal at Nuremberg in 1945.

Bonnet, Georges (1889–1973): French Radical-Socialist politician. He was Finance Minister from 1937 to 1938, then Foreign Minister in Daladier's cabinet, where he campaigned for a full policy of appeasement. He supported the Vichy regime in 1940, and left France in 1944 before the Allied D-Day invasion.

government loans and budget deficits, £15 million in 1937–8, £137 million in 1938–9. Only when the very great increases in arms spending were proposed in 1938 (£1,650 million over five years) did the situation worsen. The Chancellor of the Exchequer, Sir John Simon, opposed the increases on the grounds that 'it is impossible to escape the conclusion that we were advancing to a position in which the financial situation would get altogether out of hand' (Shay, 1977: 237). When the figure was raised to £2,000 million Simon warned the cabinet, in the same way as his German counterpart had done, of impending economic collapse. But by then Britain was too firmly committed to war preparation. Despite their fears for the worst, Treasury officials provided the funds that the services wanted as they did in France and Germany.

Finance as such was not the main constraint on the arms race. The main problem was one of resources: factory capacity, raw materials and labour. Finance only became a serious problem when the shortage of resources involved the purchase of goods from abroad, since this put great pressure on the balance of payments and on supplies of foreign exchange and gold. The critical factor here was raw materials. Britain and Germany had adequate coal supplies, but limited amounts of iron ore. France had inadequate supplies of coal, more iron ore, some bauxite for aluminium, but little else. France imported 100 per cent of its rubber, 99 per cent of its oil, 100 per cent of its copper, nickel and manganese (Young, 1978b). To increase arms output all three powers were forced to import materials from abroad. This raised the problem of how to pay for the extra imports. Some of them were paid for by liquidating investments held abroad, but this was a temporary solution. Germany used up these sources in 1936 and 1937, but Britain and France were both reluctant to prejudice their declining investment position abroad by liquidating their assets, since these investments were supposed to be a source of strength in time of war. Nor did they wish to frighten financial and trading circles too much by introducing greater government control of foreign trade. The alternative was to pay for imports by increased exports. But the problem here was that rearmament (for which imports were necessary) reduced the amount of industrial capacity available for the export industries, and produced instead a balance of payments crisis.

There were a number of ways round this dilemma. In Germany Hitler ordered the development of a vast programme of substitute production, using domestic resources to avoid having to pay for imports. In addition stringent controls were set up over gold and currency transactions to make sure that Germany could pay for what it needed abroad. Exports were subsidized and special trading agreements set up which gave Germany privileged access to raw materials. The incorporation of Austria and the occupation of the Czech lands brought additional gold and foreign exchange resources into the Reich but also involved additional expenditure in taking them over.

These were all solutions not open to the western powers, with their commitment to liberal economics and the free market, and under strong pressure from the United States after the Exchange Equalization Agreement of 1936 not to interfere with the exchange system. In France the situation was especially serious in 1936 and 1937. The flight of gold, caused by loss of confidence at home, weakened the franc and forced a series of devaluations that left the franc at a third of its 1929 value by 1938. This meant dearer imports, which made rearmament still more expensive. Nor could France benefit from increased exports, which a cheaper franc might have encouraged, because of the relative inefficiency of much of French industry and increased labour costs with the introduction of the forty-hour week in 1936. Britain's hope of expanding exports from the staple industries to pay for imports broke down because of the general crisis in world trade. The domestic recovery in Britain was fuelled by home demand rather than exports, the exact opposite of what was required to cope with rearmament. Yet the expansion of the arms sector threatened to reduce home demand and divert foreign trade away from civilian goods, which was electorally unpopular. The government could not easily compel industry and commerce to adopt strategic and military priorities, because of the strong political resistance to interference with the market. In the end the British government opted to run ever larger balance of payments deficits – £55 million in 1937–8, £70 million in 1939 – and accept all the risks that this involved in weakening Britain's economic position abroad.

The result, while not critical before 1939, was highly undesirable. Both France and Britain experienced a severe fall in gold reserves, the former in 1936–8, the latter in 1938–9. British holdings of gold fell from over £800 million in the spring of 1938 to £460 million by the outbreak of war. This was caused partly by having to pay for extra imports for rearmament, but it also reflected declining confidence by foreign investors. The lack of confidence then spread to the pound which experienced what was then considered to be a considerable drop in value against the dollar, falling from a high of $5 in February 1938 to $4.66 a year later (Overy, 1987). This involuntary devaluation increased pressure on the balance of payments even more, since it made imports more expensive, and came at a time when rearmament was diverting all available resources from exports. British and French efforts to increase the resources available for war by buying large quantities of material and equipment from the United States only made things worse. Exchange controls might at this stage have eased the difficulties, but would have invited retaliation from the United States and have slowed down the pace of rearmament. Instead Britain was forced to make the first concessions to the United States on British protection in the form of a trade agreement signed in November 1938. The western powers were caught in a vicious circle. Unable now to cut back on rearmament from fear of Germany, Italy and Japan, the western powers were creating a situation which called into question their ability to sustain a war of any length or to preserve domestic economic stability [**Doc. 16, p. 114**]. 'We are sailing', reflected a Treasury official, 'upon uncharted waters to an unknown destination' (Shay, 1977: 276).

Labour was also a critical factor in rearmament. There was no shortage of labour of a general kind. But rearmament required large numbers of skilled workers in engineering, metal-working and construction. Much of the unemployed workforce available in both Britain and France was located in staple industries, away from the main areas of arms production and lacking the skills needed by the arms industry. Skilled workers were the most likely to find employment once the economic recovery began and by 1936 were already working in a range of non-war industries, particularly motor vehicles. The difficulty lay in diverting these employed resources away from civilian or export production into arms work. In Germany the situation became serious as early as 1936. Under the Four-Year Plan efforts were made to restructure the workforce in favour of war-related sectors. Skilled labour was diverted towards war work and schemes established for retraining and apprenticeship. More women were recruited into employment; by 1939 52 per cent of all women aged 15–60 were working. But in practice the controls were difficult to enforce. German firms remained short of skilled labour up to the outbreak of war and beyond, a fact that held back the efforts to convert greater capacity to war work (Overy, 1994b).

In Britain and France labour controls, though discussed, were rejected as unworkable. Efforts were made to increase training schemes, and higher wages were used to attract labour from civilian into military industry. But this brought with it certain dangers. The removal of skilled workers from a firm might have the effect of making the less skilled workforce redundant, thereby increasing the level of unemployment, already very high. A brief slump in 1938 did some of the work for the government by releasing labour at a critical point in the rearmament effort, but not enough. Both governments favoured greater use of machinery and capital equipment which could be operated by semi-skilled or unskilled labour. Since rearmament required the large-scale production of standard weapons and components this made considerable sense. But it produced widespread resistance from the skilled workforce, who feared the effects on job security and wage levels produced by the dilution of skilled labour. In Britain the engineering workers, with recent memories of the depression, were particularly sensitive to this threat. Efforts to dilute and de-skill were therefore resisted. The unions not only feared the loss of skills but also distrusted the whole rearmament programme, which they saw as a temporary boom before the onset of a further period of recession and unemployment (Parker, 1981). Only the worsening international situation, and the promise of job guarantees after the emergency, persuaded labour to co-operate with the scheme. Labour relations in French factories were if anything more strained, soured by two or three years of lock-outs, strikes, factory occupations and wage restraint. Faced with a hostile workforce and international insecurity, French businessmen were slow to re-equip until large sums for investment were provided by the state in 1939. The Daladier government used indirect methods to push more labour towards the war industries, cutting home demand and state civilian expenditure to do so, and reversing the trend to shorter working hours initiated by the Popular Front.

REARMAMENT AND DOMESTIC POLITICS

The hostility of labour raised an important issue for all three powers. To what extent would large-scale rearmament jeopardize domestic political stability? All the states involved in the arms race were forced to face this question. Domestic political stability was equated with a stable economy and the maintenance of living standards. War preparation threatened economic stability and, it was feared, would lead to a sharpening of political conflict and greater social unrest.

There is no doubt that British rearmament, certainly in its early stages, was affected by this fear. The Conservative Party, the dominant partner in the national government, had to balance the problems of the international system against the prospect of political survival at home. Baldwin and Chamberlain had committed the party in 1935 to a programme of social expenditure and house building which they were reluctant to abandon for a rearmament programme whose full urgency was not yet apparent either to the government or the public. Labour's attitude even to this limited rearmament provoked Chamberlain to write: 'All the elements of danger are here . . . I can see that we might easily run, in no time, into a series of crippling strikes and finally the defeat of the Government and the advent of an ignorant, unprepared and heavily pledged opposition' (Feiling, 1946: 292). Though the situation never became as serious as Conservatives believed it might, their foreign policy was governed to a considerable extent by the fear of alienating labour and by anxiety over the price that might have to be paid (wage increases, union recognition, greater support for the League and so on) to win labour co-operation. Above all was the fear of creating another economic crisis as severe as 1929–31 before the general election due in 1940.

This political balancing act also had to be performed with industry. Though there was no question of businessmen preferring Labour to Conservative, there was a danger that rearmament would provoke resistance to excessive state control, government spending and labour policies. In 1935 business leaders warned Chamberlain that they would only co-operate with large-scale rearmament on their own terms. All of this put pressure on the government to tread warily with rearmament, and to seek for as long as possible a peaceful settlement of outstanding international issues.

In France the link between politics and defence spending was clear. High military expenditure had contributed to the fall of the Blum government. The centre-right Daladier government that followed the Popular Front in April 1938 was just as alarmed by the prospect that further increases in rearmament expenditure would lead to a decline in living standards and to popular unrest. From 1938 onwards Daladier ruled through decree laws, by-passing parliamentary opposition. In November 1938 a general strike was called in Paris to protest against wage cuts and increased hours, though it was defeated by firm government action [**Doc. 17, p. 114**]. The government remained very alive to the threat of widespread popular unrest. Even before the outbreak of war, using as an excuse the pact made between Germany and Russia, it moved to outlaw the French Communist Party in order to weaken domestic resistance to new labour legislation and mobilization plans (Adamthwaite, 1977).

Germany, despite the fact that it had an authoritarian government, was not immune from considerations of this kind. During 1936 and 1937 a political struggle was fought out between the party leaders, the military and German business over the future direction of the economy. The conservative groups around Schacht sought greater accommodation with the west and a return to freer trade and lower levels of arms spending. They feared that otherwise the economy would collapse beneath the strain and thereby revive the threat of communism which had so frightened German conservatives during the depression. Hitler wanted the opposite: higher levels of armaments, greater autarky and an independent foreign policy. It was this view that prevailed. Schacht was forced to resign in November 1937, and in 1938 Hitler purged the armed forces and the cabinet of opponents of his strategy, including the Foreign Minister, Constantin von Neurath, who was replaced by **Joachim von Ribbentrop**, a party stooge. There was little popular resistance to the regime after the first two years of repression. The destruction of the trade union movement in 1933 and the victimization of the two main left-wing parties, the German Communist Party and the German Social Democratic Party, undermined any prospect for organized worker opposition to low living standards and the absence of any right of collective wage bargaining. Many younger workers were attracted to a regime that reversed the years of dearth and unemployment while older workers, who had fought

Ribbentrop, Joachim von (1893–1946): A leading National Socialist spokesman on foreign affairs after 1933. He was appointed Ambassador to London in 1936, and in 1938 was appointed German Foreign Minister. Dominated by Hitler, he played little part in key decision making. He was tried at Nuremberg and sentenced to death.

fascism in the 1920s, had little stomach for a contest with national revolution, with some of whose aspirations they could also identify. In the 1960s the argument was put forward that the German working class found other ways of expressing their discontent with go-slows and veiled strikes, but although the government remained perennially sensitive to any possible threat from the factory workforce, there is no firm evidence that any movement of social or political protest emerged in the late 1930s. Instead the proportion of new National Socialist Party members drawn from the manual workforce steadily increased before the war, a shift that emphasized the growing fragmentation of what had been a strong sense of class solidarity before the slump (Mason, 1966, 1989; Overy, 1987).

It was in the western states that the problems of rearmament, finance and domestic politics were most acute. Fears of financial crisis and political unrest held Britain and France back from a substantial effort of rearmament until 1938, and encouraged both governments to explore the possibility of a settlement rather than run the risks of collapse at home. It can now be seen that the political risks were much exaggerated. Labour in both countries was strongly anti-fascist, and quite unprepared to bring governments down on the grounds of excessive military spending. If anything, sections of the left became increasingly critical of the governments for not taking firmer action at an earlier date. But nevertheless the fact remained that governments perceived rearmament as a domestic political problem. As such it had to be weighed in the scales when reaching decisions about the size and timing of the rearmament effort. By 1938–9 economic crisis appeared a very real possibility and the political dangers greater than ever. The high levels of arms spending could be sustained for only a short time, while the last unemployed resources were used up and before the balance of payments became critical. This fact pushed both western governments towards the conclusion that it would be better to take decisive action, even war, sooner rather than later. German preparations pointed to a war in the mid-1940s. For Britain and France the decisive year was 1939.

5

War Over Poland

THE AFTERMATH OF MUNICH

Détente: Name given to the efforts to scale down the Cold War from the late 1960s, but applied to any diplomatic effort to reduce tension and reach accommodation.

Anglo-German Agreement: Paper signed by Hitler and Chamberlain in the early hours of of 30 September 1938 after the Munich Conference, renouncing war between the two states and agreeing to settle issues by negotiation. This was the 'scrap of paper' Chamberlain waved when he arrived back in England later that day.

In the immediate afterglow of Munich it seemed at last that Europe was close to the general settlement Chamberlain wanted. His ambition in November 1938 was 'to arrive at a stabilisation of Europe' (Pratt, 1975: 152). There was a general sense of *détente*, and great relief at home that war had been averted. In Paris a crowd of half a million turned out to welcome Daladier back from Germany. Chamberlain was showered with gifts and letters from well-wishers. Britain and Germany signed the **Anglo-German Agreement**, followed a few weeks later by the ratification in Rome of an Anglo-Italian understanding reached the previous April. French and German negotiators in December signed a further agreement expressing mutual goodwill and respect of frontiers [**Doc. 18, p. 115**]. In January Chamberlain and his Foreign Secretary, Lord Halifax, visited Mussolini to try to reach a settlement of the Mediterranean area as a prelude to a more comprehensive agreement with Hitler on colonies and economic co-operation, which the British Foreign Office had been working on since early 1938. There even appeared the danger, though a remote one, that Britain and France might each try to reach a separate agreement with the dictators to safeguard their own interests, a fear that prompted the British to agree at last to full military discussions between the British and French general staffs, which began in March 1939.

Yet at the same time could be detected a very different mood in British and French governing circles. There had always been implicit limits to appeasement. It was now felt that the time had come to state clearly what they were. Though there was by no means unanimity on what exactly constituted these limits, there was general agreement that in 1939 they were likely to be put to the test. Evidence from both Germany and Italy, supplied in part by the German 'moderates' themselves, suggested that the dictators might carry out what the British Foreign Office called a 'mad-dog act' in the near future. It was foolhardy under these circumstances for the western powers to place much confidence in *détente*. Instead Chamberlain insisted that the pace of rearmament should not be allowed to slacken: 'it was clear that it would be madness for the country to stop rearming until we were convinced that other countries would act in the same way . . . we should relax no particle of effort' – a view that sits ill with the conventional historical image that Chamberlain was a reluctant rearmer (Shay, 1977: 233).

Both governments, however, agreed that there was not much point in contesting Germany's position in central Europe. Hitler, Halifax thought, should be allowed to 'go ahead and do what he liked' there, but he should not be allowed to trespass any further [Doc. 19, p. 115]. Switzerland, Holland and Belgium were deemed to be areas of vital interest in the west. In eastern Europe it was agreed that Britain and France should try to hold the line Poland-Romania-Yugoslavia. **Danzig** was not yet considered an essential interest. To this list was added the 'vital cord' of western communications through the Mediterranean, and with it the defence of Tunisia, Egypt, Greece and Turkey. To this end the British and French began to explore between January and March 1939 the prospect of an eastern Locarno, a collective guarantee, if possible including the Soviet Union, of the remaining frontiers of eastern Europe (Newman, 1976; Pratt, 1975).

German reaction to the Munich Agreement was quite different. Though Hitler was willing to sign expressions of goodwill with Britain and France he was privately furious at the frustration of his plans for war with Czechoslovakia. Nevertheless he came to assume that he had been given at Munich a green light for expansion in eastern Europe. This was an understandable miscalculation. German power was now a fact of life in eastern Europe. Britain and France had demonstrated in September how unwilling they were to risk war to contest this fact. Hitler came to regard them as decadent and spineless. A new arrogance entered into Germany's relations with its eastern neighbours. On 21 October 1938, less than a month after signing the Munich Agreement, Hitler ordered his generals to prepare for the elimination of the Czech state and the return of Memel to the Reich. The first stage of German imperialism, *Mitteleuropa*, now seemed within Hitler's grasp without a major war. Germany rejected Chamberlain's offer of discussions on colonies and economic agreements. Instead Germany tied the economies of eastern Europe more closely to its own. The rump state of Czechoslovakia was treated like a colony, compelled through its weakness to reach unfavourable economic agreements with Germany. The integrity of the Czech state was undermined by deliberate German efforts to encourage Slovak separatism. On 15 March 1939 the Czech President was forced to invite German troops to enter Czechoslovakia on the pretext that it was now ungovernable and faced with incipient civil war. The Third Reich occupied Bohemia and Moravia under a protectorate, and Slovakia became a satellite state. On

Danzig: Ancient German city declared a 'free city' under the League of Nations in the Versailles Settlement in June 1919. By 1933 its parliament was dominated by local National Socialists who made life difficult for the Polish minority in the city and demanded union with Hitler's Germany.

21 March Lithuania was forced to return Memel to German hands. A few weeks later Hitler resolved to settle accounts with Poland at some stage during 1939.

German relations with Poland had been distant but cordial since the signing of the German-Polish Non-Aggression Treaty in 1934. Polish foreign policy was concerned chiefly with avoiding any commitment either to Germany or the Soviet Union which might involve Poland in a future conflict. Spasmodic German attempts to achieve closer links with the Poles broke down on this doctrine of an independent foreign policy. After Munich the German tone changed. It was hoped in Berlin that Poland would be drawn naturally into the German orbit. Poland was asked to give up rights in Danzig which, though nominally a Free City under a League of Nations commission, had been run by a National Socialist city government since 1933. In return Poland would receive guarantees of its integrity from Germany. In January 1939 Hitler met the Polish Foreign Minister, Colonel **Josef Beck**, and added the demand for German access across the **Polish Corridor** between East Prussia and the Reich, a strip of land granted to Poland in 1919 to ensure it access to the sea. The Poles refused to consider the suggestions. The demand for Danzig, said Beck, 'must inevitably lead to conflict' (Newman, 1976: 158). The occupation of Czechoslovakia and the cession of Memel made the Polish position much weaker; German demands became more insistent and uncompromising but the Polish government remained adamant. In secret Hitler revealed his true plans for Poland to his generals: 'It is not Danzig that is at stake. For us it is a matter of expanding our living space in the east and making food supplies secure'. Polish economic and labour resources, like those of Czechoslovakia and Austria, were needed to build up German strength for the great war in the future [**Doc. 20, p. 116**]. Hitler was confident that this could be achieved without a general war. His anglophobe Foreign Minister, Ribbentrop, suggested that Britain and France were waning powers, who would seek any solution, however shoddy, to avoid having to fight. This belief played a vital part in Hitler's decision to compel Poland, by force if necessary, to come within the German sphere.

This, in the end, was to be a costly miscalculation. The German occupation of Prague was confirmation, if confirmation were needed, that Hitler could not be restrained by paper guarantees. It forced both the French and British governments to give firm expression to their strategy of containing the dictator powers, which had been slowly taking shape since Munich. It would be wrong to see Prague as the point at which enfeebled appeasers were finally compelled by an outraged public to stand up to the dictators. Both before and after Prague, western strategy was guided by the desire to reach a European settlement on British and French terms, backed up by rising military power to be used only at the point where vital British and French

Beck, Josef (1894–1944): Polish soldier and politician who became Polish Foreign Minister in 1932. He was determined to resist all political demands from either Germany or the Soviet Union and preferred war in 1939 rather than make concessions.

Polish Corridor: Narrow strip of land carved out of the former German province of East Prussia to allow the newly formed Polish state access to the sea. The corridor divided eastern and western parts of Germany and became a key issue on treaty revision in the 1930s.

Plate 1 Neville Chamberlain reviews SS troops on his arrival for the Munich Conference, 29 September 1938. To his left is the British Ambassador, Sir Nevile Henderson, to his right the German Foreign Minister, Joachim von Ribbentrop.

Source: Time & Life Pictures/Getty Images

Plate 2 The centre of Nuremberg during the annual party gathering in the city. By the late 1930s popular enthusiasm for Hitler was widespread. Pageantry played an important part in cementing support for the regime.

Source: Time & Life Pictures/Getty Images

Plate 3 One of many Republican posters from the Spanish Civil War fought between July 1936 and March 1939. Here the *Unión General de Trabajadores* (UGT) shows fascism sowing not seeds but graves.

Source: Mary Evans Picture Library

Plate 4 A poster from the Soviet collectivization drive of the early 1930s. Stalin recognized that defence of the new communist state depended critically on economic modernization. Tractor factories were set up so that they could be converted to tank production.

Source: Elkin, Vasilii, 'Every Kolkhoz Member, Every Brigade, Every MPS Must Know the Plan of Bolshevik Sowing'. International Poster Gallery: www.internationalposter.com

Plate 5 The Japanese expansion in China in the 1930s was carried out with great brutality. Here inhabitants of Nanking clear up bomb damage after a Japanese air attack in November 1937, prior to the capture of the city and the killing of an estimated 260,000–350,000 of the population.

Source: SV-Bilderdienst

Plate 6 Konrad Henlein (1898–1945) leader of the Sudeten German Party, which was founded to campaign for autonomy for the Germans living in the Czech state. The movement came to model itself on Hitler's National Socialist Party.

Source: Time & Life Pictures/Getty Images

Plate 7 Franklin Delano Roosevelt, President of the United States from 1932 to his death in 1945, on the campaign trail. He was very sensitive to popular opinion and hesitated to do more to stop the international crisis because of the strong isolationist views of many Americans.

Source: Mary Evans Picture Library

Plate 8 A Supermarine Spitfire in flight. The RAF legendary fighter, first developed in the mid-1930s, became the mainstay of Britain's fighter force during the war. British rearmament was concentrated on air defence in the years before 1939 because of widespread popular fear of bombing.

Source: Coloured photograph in 'Our Air force', Mary Evans Picture Library

interests were at stake. It was not until the spring of 1939 that the limits of this policy were finally reached. Rightly or wrongly, Britain and France now saw the problem in terms of their interests as great powers, and not in terms of 'saving' eastern Europe.

In the weeks after Prague the British and French searched for some way of making this situation clear to Hitler. Since they had been exploring the possibility of guarantees in eastern Europe for some months, it was decided that a firm gesture should now be made in that direction, particularly as there now existed the possibility that Poland might be pushed into the arms of Germany if the west held back. Chamberlain argued for a four-power declaration, including the Soviet Union, to guarantee Polish independence. Poland was unhappy with any agreement that left it dependent on Soviet goodwill, and Stalin anyway rejected what he saw as western efforts to get the Soviet Union, in his words, 'to pull the chestnuts out of the fire' (Degras, 1951–3: vol. 2, 320). However, following the German occupation of Prague, Chamberlain searched for some way of showing Hitler that he could go no further. After obtaining secret, but false, intelligence that Poland was about to be attacked, he decided to use the Polish issue as his signal to Hitler. On 31 March Britain gave a public guarantee to Poland [**Doc. 21, p. 117**] to intervene in the event of any threat to Polish independence, though it carried the rider, privately expressed, that the Poles 'would not indulge in provocative behaviour or stupid obstinacy either generally or in particular as regards Danzig' (Newman, 1976: 202). Beck had not expected it and distrusted British motives. Poland accepted the guarantee on grounds of what Beck called 'insurance'.

The British saw the **Polish Guarantee** as a prelude to a more general set of alliances. From a policy of no formal commitment Britain embarked on a scrambled search for allies in the Balkans and the Mediterranean. Romania was regarded as a key power, and when the French government, delighted to have got an eastern European commitment from Britain for the first time (but far from happy that Poland, with its authoritarian and anti-semitic government, should be the beneficiary), asked for a guarantee of Romanian frontiers too, the British agreed. Neither Romania nor Yugoslavia would be drawn into any effort to encircle Germany, however, and instead moved closer to the Axis powers. The only real successes for British diplomacy were closer ties with Greece and Turkey, which were both alarmed at the sudden change in the balance of power in the Balkans following the occupation of Czechoslovakia.

Mussolini had been as disturbed by the German coup in Prague as the western powers. His initial reaction was one of hurt pride that his fellow dictator could leave him as ignorant of his intentions as everyone else. There was even talk of moving closer to Britain and France. Instead Mussolini,

Polish Guarantee: Name given to the announcement by Neville Chamberlain in the House of Commons on 31 March 1939 that Poland's sovereignty would be guaranteed by Britain. France pledged similar support a few days later, but a firm Anglo-Polish Treaty was only signed on 25 August, a few days before the German invasion.

backed up by Fascist Party leaders, decided to embark on his own foreign policy initiatives to show Hitler that he, too, was capable of taking on the inert power of Britain and France. On 30 March he ordered the occupation of Albania, which had been for some time an Italian satellite in all but name, and announced that the Balkans and eastern Mediterranean should now be regarded as the Italian sphere of influence. Hitler was content to see Mussolini turn southwards, since it would occupy the British and French while he settled the Polish question. Somewhat to his surprise Mussolini then proposed a close military alliance between the two powers which was signed on 22 May in Berlin. The 'Pact of Steel', as it was called, required each power to help the other unconditionally in the event of war. Mussolini justified this commitment on the grounds that it gave a formal and equal partnership in place of the growing inferiority that had characterized Italian relations with Germany since the *Anschluss* (Knox, 1983).

The Pact of Steel upset British and French calculations that Mussolini might be detached from Germany as part of the strategy of containing Hitler. It confirmed French mistrust and hostility towards Italy, and hardened the military collaboration between the two western states. Close co-operation had begun following Chamberlain's statement on 6 February committing Britain to assist France on the continent. This commitment was a turning point in the European situation in 1939. Britain's isolation from Europe since the 1920s was finally ended, and France had the promise of an alliance without which any firmer line against Germany was out of the question. Staff talks were started in March 1939, and the British Chiefs-of-Staff drew up what was called a 'War Plan' based on the likely international situation in 1939 [**Doc. 22, p. 117**]. On 26 April Britain reintroduced conscription, and the volunteer Territorial Army was doubled in size. Over the summer months joint planning was extended to all areas of a possible war. It did not involve Poland, except to the extent that Poland's fifty-four divisions were reckoned to be a useful addition to the Allies' strength. In May **General Gamelin**, French Commander-in-Chief, promised the Polish government that France would begin an offensive within three weeks of a German attack, but he privately agreed with the British that nothing could be done in the short term to save Poland. The British and French plan was based on preventing a German offensive westwards until the sea blockade and bombing had so worn down German capacity to wage war that a swift ground attack would finish the job, a strategy dangerously rooted in the victorious war of 1914–18. By the time the British agreed to a full alliance with Poland on 25 August 1939, preparations for war in the immediate future were well advanced (Bond, 1980; Howard, 1972).

Why did Britain and France choose to risk a major war in the summer of 1939? The popular explanation was that war was thrust upon them by the

Gamelin, General Maurice (1872–1958): French general who became Chief-of-Staff in 1936 and oversaw the rearmament of France in the late 1930s. He was replaced in the middle of the Battle of France in 1940 by Marshal Maxime Weygand. The Vichy regime put him on trial and he was later deported to Germany.

insatiable appetites of the Axis powers, which public opinion in Britain and France was no longer willing to tolerate. Against their will, so the argument went, the appeasers were forced to accept the widespread revulsion against fascism and to stand at the head of a crusade against the totalitarian powers. It is certainly the case that political differences at home were suppressed by a rising tide of national sentiment that made it much easier for both governments to make clear after March their determination to defend their vital interests by force. There was also much anti-fascist idealism which could be used to bolster a policy of greater firmness and forge a consensus willing, if need be, to embrace war, despite the grim forebodings of its apocalyptic character. But the evidence suggests that British and French leaders were aware sooner than this that they might have to take action to restrain Hitler, and had been building up towards that conclusion since Munich. In February Chamberlain wrote to his sister that he was now able to take 'a "firmer" line in public' (Overy and Wheatcroft, 1998: 94). At least some of the change in public opinion was engineered by the government, and not the other way around. Both populations had to be persuaded over the summer that Danzig was a cause worth fighting for where the Sudetenland had not been. There remained large minorities in both countries who were never reconciled to a firmer line or the risk of war, but in neither case was their influence powerful enough to force governments to seek a peaceful solution. For the rest there developed a mood of growing fatalism about the inevitability of war.

Danzig was not, of course, the issue, though it could be used as a rallying cry to mobilize public opinion against German aggression. The Polish issue gave a moral gloss to what was in fact a decision about when was the best time to fight for Britain and France, not for Poland. If this seems a harsh judgement, it is a realistic one. If Britain and France had not put themselves in a position in which, rightly or wrongly, they felt able to run the risk of declaring war on their terms, then Poland might well have been sacrificed as had Czechoslovakia, public opinion or no. There were prominent politicians on both sides of the Channel who thought this the most reasonable course both before, and even after, the outbreak of war. Their number included the French Foreign Minister, Georges Bonnet, but not, as is often suggested, either Chamberlain or Daladier. The British and French decision to risk war in 1939 was based on what was perceived to be a temporarily more favourable set of international and domestic circumstances, reinforced by the economic, military and moral necessity of waging war sooner rather than later. The alternative to not fighting, if Germany refused to back down, was to sacrifice this opportunity and to forfeit their status as first-class powers. 'France', observed Daladier in November 1938, had to choose 'between a slow decline or a renaissance through effort' (Mommsen and Kettenacker, 1983: 247).

During the course of 1939 a number of new elements of particular value to the western states entered into their calculations. The British Dominions, which had all (except New Zealand) favoured appeasement up to and beyond the Munich crisis, now moved towards giving positive support to the mother country in the event of a European conflict. The rallying of the empire was regarded by Chamberlain as a factor of exceptional importance. The French Empire was also seen as a source of strength. The Colonial Minister Georges Mandel talked of 'le salut par l'empire' – salvation through the empire. Efforts were made to mobilize manpower and resources as had been done during the First World War, when over 600,000 colonial troops had been raised. New armies were raised in the colonies of North and West Africa, though not without occasional protest, and by 1940 there were ten colonial divisions in France, with over 100,000 conscripted from West Africa alone. The raw materials and foodstuffs of the Empire were ruthlessly requisitioned, although efforts to expand industrial output in colonial areas were frustrated by shortages of skilled manpower and capital and the hostility of metropolitan industry to the idea of developing rival sources of production in the colonies (Thomas, 2005).

More important still, the United States drew perceptibly closer to the western European powers, despite the formal commitment to neutrality. Chamberlain found Roosevelt 'wary but helpful' (Pratt, 1975: 187). While keeping the isolationists at bay, Roosevelt tried to find ways of supplying Britain and France with arms and raw materials without abandoning neutrality. The cash-and-carry principle incorporated in the Neutrality Act allowed the western powers to collect non-war materials without undue difficulty. The long lists of aviation equipment which the French and British drew up after Munich were a different matter. Only the insistence of the American air forces that this was a convenient way to get someone else to pay for the early stages of America's own rearmament persuaded the President to accept the orders, although to do so meant a confrontation with Congress (Haight, 1981). What was more important to the Allies was the fact that America, whether it liked it or not, was assuming more of the responsibility in the Far East for keeping Japan in check. Japanese foreign policy was constricted by the long-drawn-out Chinese war and by fear of the Soviet Union, with whom Japan found itself in armed conflict during 1939 along the Manchurian-Siberian border over disputed territory (a military clash on a large scale, overshadowed by the larger crisis in the west). Ribbentrop's attempt to get the Japanese to sign a formal military alliance early in 1939 was rejected in Tokyo for fear of alienating the other major Pacific powers while Japan was still fighting the war in China.

The United States would not, on the other hand, give any kind of formal commitment to the Allies. This for Chamberlain was the ideal solution. As long as America confined itself to supplying economic resources, Britain and France would not be too dependent on the United States when it came to confronting Hitler. If Britain and France waited longer, then economic dependence would be much greater, and America might well set political conditions, such as colonial self-government and an end to protection, as a price for further help. This would make explicit the decline of Britain and France as great powers and produce the same long-term effect as the failure to confront Germany. These were devious, even wrong-headed, calculations; so devious that some Americans believed that the British and French were secretly planning to build an anti-American economic bloc in Europe with Hitler's co-operation, a solution that had certainly been voiced at times in official circles, though never seriously considered. In their turn the British, with some justice, harboured the suspicion that if the United States became more involved in Europe's affairs, the effect on the Empire would be very damaging. It was perceived to be more in the Allies' interests to keep America at a distance as a friendly, rich neutral while they faced up to Germany themselves (Mommsen and Kettenacker, 1983; Reynolds, 1981).

The second factor that weighed heavily in the scales in 1939 was the relative shift in the military balance in Europe. By the autumn of 1939 both Britain and France were much stronger than they had been at the time of Munich. As had been intended, the great rearmament programmes were now bearing fruit. British rearmament was geared to reach a peak in 1939–40. The air plans laid down in 1936 had aimed at this date; so too did the four-year plan outlined in the Defence White Paper in 1936. The air defence of Britain, based on fast monoplane fighters and the introduction of radar, was near completion in 1939. When Chamberlain asked the head of the Military Supply Board in July 1938 when he could expect armaments roughly on equal terms with Germany he got the reply: 'in a year' (Feiling, 1946: 35). Maurice Hankey, Chairman of the Defence Requirements Committee, gave Chamberlain the same date, mid-1939, when Britain could begin to feel secure militarily.

French rearmament was at last in full swing too. British and French tank and aircraft production exceeded German by the summer of 1939 and was known to do so through military intelligence. General Gamelin had told the French Foreign Minister the year before that France would need two years before it could mount a serious offensive against Germany, but in 1939 he trusted that France could keep Germany bottled up behind the Maginot Line while the final preparations for offensive strategy were completed. He hoped that a German war with Poland would allow 'the time necessary to put on a war footing all Franco-British forces' (Boyce, 1989: 157). Although there was still widespread public concern at western unpreparedness, there was a growing realization in government circles that western strength was now more evenly weighted against German. These were compelling arguments. Chamberlain hoped that the western allies' forces would be sufficiently strong to deter Germany altogether from risking an armed confrontation. But whether the western powers fought or only deterred Hitler, the favourable military balance could not be expected to last. To a greater extent than Germany, the western states were trapped in a military timetable of their own choosing. This created the necessity of confronting Hitler at what they judged to be the best moment.

This growing confidence was augmented by a stream of intelligence information from Germany and Italy which suggested that both powers faced growing economic crises and would not be able to risk, let alone sustain, a major conflict. The British military attaché in Berlin supplied evidence that Germany would not be ready for a major war for a number of years, since it did not yet have sufficient control over the newly won resources of central and eastern Europe [Doc. 23, p. 118]. These reports confirmed the assessment by the Economic Intelligence department that the German economy was now stretched taut and might collapse with the first push. This view fitted well with the Allied strategy of blockade and economic warfare. The prospects for actually defeating Germany appeared to be better than they had been since the mid-1930s, but could not be expected to last. It was thought that German strength would increase, once it was magnified by the use of eastern European resources which would save Germany from the effects of blockade, while that of the Allies would relatively decline. By 1942, it was argued, the situation might have deteriorated so far as to make a declaration of war impossible.

Nor were the Allies immune from the prospect of economic crisis. Though they were certain that their current financial and commercial strength was greater than Germany's, a high level of readiness for war could not be sustained without the real prospect of economic and political difficulties at home. The British Chancellor of the Exchequer urged this view throughout the summer. Oliver Stanley, the President of the Board of Trade, drew the conclusion that 'there would come a moment which, on a balance of our financial strength and our strength in armaments, was the best time for war to break out' (Shay, 1977: 280). The danger of inflation fuelled by a high level of government borrowing was expected to develop from the autumn of 1939 onwards as unemployed resources were gradually used up. The run on gold and foreign exchange reserves could not be sustained indefinitely without stringent controls which might well prejudice important parts of the arms programme, and would almost certainly have made it difficult to get further American co-operation. If the 'fourth arm of defence' were to weigh in the scales at all, then it was clear that it would be better for the Allies to use the threat of war, or war itself, in 1939 or early 1940 at the latest (Parker, 1983).

All of these were pressing arguments for confronting Hitler. Of course they did not make war inevitable. If Hitler had not put pressure on Poland, war would not have been necessary at all, at least not in September 1939. Nor would war have been the outcome if Hitler had agreed to accept the conditions laid down by the Allies for a settlement. There were many opportunities extended to Germany to adopt a position acceptable to Britain and France, broadly those laid down at Munich. But in 1939 the Allies made it clear that any settlement had to be within those terms, which to the Germans was tantamount to an admission that they enjoyed their great-power status only at the behest of Britain and France. This was the solution that the western states would have preferred: to use their armed might to force Hitler to back down without the horrors of another great war. No one, least of all Chamberlain, wanted such a war; but he accepted the possibility of war with gloomy dignity, torn between his conviction that in an ideal world compromise was always possible and his reluctant acceptance that in practice it was not. Right up to the last, every effort was made to get Hitler to see the reality of his situation and the futility of war.

THE SOVIET FACTOR

Diplomatic reality meant something very different to Hitler than it did to Chamberlain. Hitler had predicted in November 1937 that Britain and France would make no serious effort to save eastern Europe. Events had borne out this conclusion. By March 1939 he had achieved almost all that he wanted for the first stage of German expansion. It seemed both unlikely and unreasonable to expect the western powers to fight for Poland when they had forgone everything else. 'Our task,' he explained in May 1939, 'is to isolate Poland. There must be no simultaneous conflict with the western powers' (Overy, 1984: 90). To make sure of this outcome, German leaders actively sought to create a set of diplomatic circumstances which they felt would almost certainly secure non-intervention.

The strategy chosen was to neutralize, if possible, either the Soviet Union or Britain, or both. Ribbentrop and the German Foreign Office explored the first possibility, while Goering pursued the second. The British gambit was not played with any urgency or consistency, since Germany did not want to reach another firm agreement as it had at Munich, unless the terms amounted to a free hand in eastern Europe. Rather the object was to persuade Britain of the reasonableness of the German case and, through German willingness to talk, to place Britain in a position of uncertainty until it could be faced with a swift *coup* in Poland which could not be effectively reversed.

In all this Goering played a calculated role as a man of greater moderation than Hitler, whose good offices might be used to make Hitler more conciliatory. There were few on the British side who took Goering's role very seriously, though it did have the effect, as Hitler and Goering hoped, of confusing the moderates in the British government in the weeks before the outbreak of war as they weighed up the flow of conflicting information emanating from Berlin (Overy, 1984).

For Hitler the Soviet strategy was far more important, for it avoided a repeat of the **July Crisis** of 1914 when Russia and the western powers could not be kept apart by German and Austrian diplomacy. If the Soviet Union could be neutralized, then the danger in the west would recede. Otherwise there existed the threat, made clear by the Franco-British efforts to construct a four-power agreement with Poland and Russia in March 1939, of a revival of the pre-1914 entente against Germany. This fear had first become apparent before the Munich Conference when it seemed possible that Stalin would intervene in Czechoslovakia if the French would honour their pledge of military assistance. The evidence about the Soviet Union's real intentions in September 1938 is still inconclusive, since some of the central archives on the issue are still closed. No effort was made to co-ordinate French or Soviet policy (the Soviet Union was not even invited to the Munich Conference). The diplomatic evidence suggests that the Soviet side did not want to risk war over the Czech crisis either, but did not want to accept any of the responsibility for leaving the Czechs in the lurch. For a time it seems the Czech leadership, and Beneš in particular, placed too much faith in the prospect of Soviet assistance. He thought that any assistance might be limited to military supplies and aircraft, like Soviet intervention in the Spanish Civil War. There is evidence that a limited mobilization of Soviet forces occurred in the late summer, but this may well have been directed at the Poles, as a warning not to invade Czechoslovakia if the Germans did. There was little prospect that the Poles would ever have allowed the Red Army to cross its territory to aid Czechoslovakia, though the Romanian government seems to have been willing to allow Soviet aircraft and Soviet army units a corridor to pass through. The Soviet side did assure the Czechs that if France fought for them, and Britain too, then they would honour the agreement to protect them, but Stalin must have known very well that this was a highly unlikely outcome and could afford to look more generous than Soviet foreign policy actually was. In the end Beneš seems to have decided that with only half-hearted promises, conflict with the resurgent German armed forces was not worth the risk (Steiner, 1999; Lukes, 1993).

Both sides at the Munich Conference drew their own conclusions about Soviet motives. The Soviet factor was an important one in German plans to extend their influence further into eastern Europe. In the spring of 1939 the

July Crisis: The month-long diplomatic crisis following the assassination of the Habsburg Archduke Franz Ferdinand on 28 June 1914 in Sarajevo. The crisis paved the way for the outbreak of the First World War.

German side made exploratory contacts with the Soviet Union, encouraged by Ribbentrop, German Foreign Minister. The possibility of a Soviet-German *rapprochement* had not escaped the British and French, who regarded **Stalin** as an opportunist, just like Hitler. In the spring of 1939 they, too, began to send feelers out to the Soviet Union to see whether Stalin could be won over to a policy of containing German ambitions through a broad diplomatic front in eastern Europe.

From a position of diplomatic isolation in 1938 Stalin found himself courted by both the Axis and the western powers. He trusted neither side. Hitler's Germany was the sworn enemy of Bolshevism. Britain and France were regarded as the major imperialist and capitalist powers, capable of luring the Soviet Union into a war to suit their own ends [**Doc. 24, p. 119**]. Stalin's chief object was to avoid Soviet involvement in any major war at all costs. Soviet diplomats were instructed early in 1939 to try to revive collective security at just the time when international confidence in collective security had completely evaporated. When Britain and France began to make approaches in March 1939, Stalin switched to a more active interpretation of collective action by offering in April a three-way military alliance – the Soviet Union, France and Britain – directed against further German expansion. Under the proposed Soviet terms all the territories from the Baltic States to the Black Sea were to be given guarantees of direct military assistance by all three powers. The Soviet Foreign Minister, **Maxim Litvinov**, doubted that such an alliance was workable after witnessing western behaviour at Munich. On 3 May 1939 he was replaced by Stalin's close ally, **Vyacheslav Molotov**, who was instructed to continue to press the west for a serious military alliance. Up to that point Soviet leaders could not discount a German drive eastward directed at Soviet territory. A military alliance with the west was a genuine attempt to avert the clash with fascism.

The west responded to the offer of an alliance with limited enthusiasm. Chamberlain did not like having to woo communists: 'I must confess the most profound distrust of Russia, and I distrust her motives, which seem to me to have little connection with our idea of liberty, and to be concerned only with getting every one else by the ears' (Feiling, 1946: 403). The French were more eager, for there existed a long tradition of Franco-Russian co-operation, but even Daladier feared that war might hasten communist domination of western Europe: 'Cossacks will rule Europe!' (Mommsen and Kettenacker, 1983: 248). This fear was echoed by the British Ambassador in Moscow, who thought that Stalin was trying to turn Germany against the west so that the ensuing conflict would weaken all the capitalist powers to his advantage. This was certainly consistent with what is now known of Soviet thinking. The regime accepted the Leninist argument that war was a symptom of capitalism in decline, and hoped that the capitalist powers

Stalin (Joseph Dzhugashvili) (1878–1953): Georgian Marxist who became Commissar for Nationalities in the first Bolshevik government in November 1917. In 1922 he was appointed General Secretary of the party and used this position to help him to establish a personal dictatorship in the Soviet Union from the 1930s to the 1950s.

Litvinov, Maxim (1876–1951): Russian Bolshevik politician and diplomat. He was appointed Foreign Minister in 1930 but replaced in March 1939. He later served as Soviet Ambassador to the United States from 1941 to 1943.

Molotov, Vyacheslav (1890–1986): Bolshevik politician and close associate of Stalin, whose secretariat he served in the 1920s. He was made Chairman of the Council of People's Commissars in 1930 (Prime Minister) until 1941, and was also Commissar for Foreign Affairs from 1939 until 1949.

would fight among themselves, leaving the Soviet Union free to 'take action last' – mopping up what was left of a battered Europe for the communist cause. In October 1939 Stalin told the Comintern leadership that he was indifferent to whether the democratic or fascist states prevailed as long as 'they weaken each other'. Stalin's priority was to avoid war at all costs if it meant bearing the brunt of the fighting in order to save the capitalist states.

For the west the pursuit of a Soviet agreement produced more practical problems too. It threatened to alienate the eastern European countries that Britain was trying to win over to the diplomatic front against Germany, and carried the additional danger that Poland and Spain, both key countries in western calculations in 1939, might be driven into the arms of Hitler. Nevertheless, there were strong pressures in both states, but particularly France, to undertake firm negotiations with the Soviet side. The French Foreign Minister thought that a Soviet alliance was the only chance of preventing a European war, as did Churchill in Britain. Chamberlain and Halifax hoped that talks with the Soviet Union, even if they produced nothing positive, could be used to buy support for their foreign policy from the British left and from the trade unions, where there were loud voices for closer ties with the Soviet side. Even the military chiefs favoured discussions, despite the fact that they did not rate the Red Army very highly after the purges of the Soviet military leadership in 1937 and 1938. They argued that discussions might have the effect of restraining Germany in eastern Europe, without the need for a firm Soviet military alliance at all (Manne, 1974).

Talks continued throughout the summer, though both sides complained endlessly about the obduracy and deviousness of the other. In August the Soviet side insisted on full military discussions before any more progress could be made. Again the west showed what Molotov later condemned as a 'dilatory' attitude (Degras, 1951–3: vol. 2, 365). The British delegation was sent on a long trip by sea instead of by air. When it arrived the Soviet negotiators, all top military and political figures, found that the British had sent a junior representative, who had no powers to negotiate and sign an agreement. This slight deeply offended Soviet leaders. It was soon discovered that the western delegations had no real plans for the military alliance, and had not even secured agreement for the passage of Soviet forces across Poland to fight the German army. The discussions, which had begun on 12 August 1939, broke up after three days and were not revived [**Doc. 25, p. 119**].

The failure of the Franco-British approach to the Soviet Union did not in the end alter the terms of the crisis over Poland, for neither the British nor the French were confident that Stalin would have been a trustworthy or militarily useful ally. What the British most wanted, Soviet support for Poland in case of German aggression, was unrealistic. The Poles did not want a Soviet guarantee under any circumstances, for they knew that the Soviet Union wanted to win back the lands lost in the Soviet-Polish war of 1920. The Soviet side, on the other hand, did not want to guarantee Poland alone, for they believed that the British and French would leave the Soviet Union to bear the brunt of the fighting in the east. This was not an unfounded fear. In July 1939 Gamelin wrote: 'we have every interest in the war beginning in the east and becoming a general conflict only little by little' (Boyce, 1989: 87). Stalin wanted firm guarantees that the west would share the risk of war by being in earnest about a three-way alliance. What Soviet leaders wanted, the French Ambassador wrote to Paris on 21 August, was 'simple concrete decisions quickly' (Buffotot, 1982: 355). This was something the west was never in a position to supply given the prevailing attitude towards Soviet communism. Both western states decided that the Soviet Union was militarily unprepared and politically unreliable and that Hitler could be confronted without it.

The ideological gulf between National Socialism and Soviet communism seemed in 1939 even greater than the divisions between the Soviet Union and the western democracies. This did not prevent German officials from trying to establish discussions with the Soviet Union during 1939 to try to prevent any new alliance front against them, but it did mean that Soviet officials remained highly sceptical about German intentions long after the initial contacts were made in May. It is not clear that the German side had any particular plan in view, but on 30 May the German Ambassador in Moscow was told by the Foreign Office that 'we have now decided to undertake definite negotiations with the Soviet Union' (Ulam, 1968: 272). It takes two sides to negotiate, and the Soviet contacts refused to be drawn. Molotov dismissed German approaches as 'superficial' and 'noncommittal', as 'some sort of game' (Roberts, 1995: 73–5). Far from reacting favourably to the idea of a German-Soviet entente, Soviet leaders retained a healthy distrust [**Doc. 26, p. 120**]. Not until early August, with the Polish crisis deepening, did Ribbentrop finally make a concrete offer. The Soviet side was told that a general political agreement was possible over eastern Europe, even a non-aggression pact. The reaction in Moscow was one of disbelief. Not until 17 August, when it was clear that the talks with the French and British had reached stalemate, did Molotov finally agree to talk.

By this stage the German negotiators were desperate for an agreement in order to complete the diplomatic rout of western policies of 'encirclement', and to make certain that the Polish war could be localized. On 19 August Ribbentrop was invited to Moscow, but not to come before the 26th. Hitler telegraphed Stalin personally to ask for an earlier meeting. Stalin replied within two hours agreeing to a visit on the 21st. Ribbentrop flew to Moscow where he was greeted with conspicuously greater warmth than the British and French ten days before. Soviet leaders were now in an unexpected

German-Soviet Non-Aggression Pact: Agreement between Germany and the USSR signed on 23 August 1939 agreeing not to resort to war. The treaty also contained a trade agreement and a secret protocol dividing eastern Europe into spheres of influence. It was followed by a firm agreement on the new frontier in Poland signed on 28 September 1939.

position of being able to exploit Hitler's haste and grab new opportunities in eastern Europe, but they were still anxious to avoid war. The **German-Soviet Non-Aggression Pact** agreed between Molotov and Ribbentrop on 23 August supplied everything both sides wanted. Hitler got Soviet neutrality and, he hoped, an end to prospects of western intervention; Stalin got a non-aggression pact, a trade treaty which promised German weapons and machinery in return for Soviet materials, and a secret protocol which granted an agreed sphere of influence in Finland, the Baltic States, eastern Poland and the Romanian province of Bessarabia, all of them territories of the former Tsarist Empire [**Doc. 27, p. 121**]. The news of the pact, but not of the secret protocol, was published on 24 August. When Hitler heard confirmation he was overjoyed. 'Now Europe is mine,' he is said to have shouted.

Did the Soviet factor make any difference to the outbreak of war? It certainly had the effect of convincing Hitler that the western powers could not now intervene to save Poland and that a general European war would be averted. On 22 August he told his generals: 'war between Poland and Germany will remain localised . . . England and France will make threats, but will not declare war' (Overy, 1984: 90). The news of the pact two days later made it seem a lesser risk than the one he had run the year before in the Czech crisis. To the western states the pact proved what they had already suspected about Soviet unreliability, but since their strategy was already based on the assumption that the Soviet Union would remain isolated from the conflict or would be of little military assistance even if it joined it, the pact made much less difference to the decision to go to war than Hitler supposed. If anything, the pact meant that the Soviet Union would be free to contain Japan in the east, weakening the anti-Comintern states to British and French advantage. Italy's response was equally favourable to Britain and France. Mussolini was surprised and dismayed by the pact, which he had not been told about in advance. He did not want to be dragged into war over the Polish issue, but the Pact of Steel signed four months before obliged him to give Germany assistance. In the end he found an escape mechanism: as the price for Italian help his German ally was sent a request for economic assistance far beyond anything Germany could reasonably supply. Hitler understood Mussolini's purpose but was unconcerned about Italian defection. The Italian Foreign Minister, **Count Ciano**, made sure that the western states discovered the change in Italian policy. The western allies no longer had to fear a simultaneous conflict with all three Axis states. Of course if Britain and France had reached a firm agreement with the Soviet Union Hitler might well have held back from invading Poland and have resorted to diplomatic and economic pressure instead. But this was a remote possibility in the circumstances of 1939 because the west had chosen Poland, most anti-Soviet of the eastern states, as the frontier where Hitler was to be stopped.

Ciano, Count Galeazzo (1903–44): Mussolini's son-in-law who was appointed Italian Foreign Minister in 1936, replacing Mussolini. After Italy's surrender to the Allies in September 1943 he was arrested by the German-backed fascist regime set up in northern Italy and shot in 1944.

THE OUTBREAK OF WAR

The outbreak of a general European war in September 1939 had its immediate origins in the illusions and miscalculations over the Polish crisis. A number of historians have argued that this was Hitler's intention all along – to use the Polish crisis as an opportunity to wage war against the two western states. Gerhard Weinberg has suggested that Hitler reached the decision to move west after the Munich crisis, in order to secure his rear before embarking on the war to the east (Weinberg, 1980). The move to a general war can also be seen as an act of desperation, to fight the west in order to avoid facing up to the economic contradictions of the great rush for high levels of arms (Tooze, 2006). Neither argument stands up to scrutiny. It is true that Hitler after Munich had no illusions about Franco-British hostility, and that he did not rule out the possibility of war at some point, but the evidence surrounding the Polish crisis makes it clear that this was supposed to be the successful small war he was denied the year before. He was convinced that Poland could be isolated, and made no serious military preparations for any campaign against the west. The potential problems of rearmament certainly explain why Poland was so important to Hitler – after conquest large supplies of coal, iron ore and other materials were Germanized – but there is again no concrete evidence that Hitler was swayed by short-term economic issues into risking major war, an outcome that could only have exacerbated the situation rather than resolve it.

The existing evidence is much more consistent with the idea that Poland was to be subjugated by a short, sharp campaign or, if the Polish government abandoned resistance, be drawn fully into the German orbit. By the late summer Hitler was determined on the latter course. There were moments of hesitation before the German-Soviet Pact was signed, and when Britain and France reiterated their military support for Poland on 25–6 August. Hitler was also said to be deeply affected by the news from Italy that Mussolini was not going to risk war (though the German military did not regard Italian assistance with much confidence). But in the end none of these considerations weighed with Hitler, who had convinced himself that his assessment of western vacillation was the right one. 'I have at last decided to do without the opinions of people who have misinformed me on a dozen occasions,' he told von Ribbentrop on 31 August, 'I shall rely on my own judgement.' Even if the western powers reacted to the invasion of Poland, Hitler reasoned that they could not and would not help it militarily (which proved to be true) and would make mere gestures designed to save face, as they had done in 1938. He persisted with this view right through to the point in October 1939 when he made what he regarded as a magnanimous gesture of peace in the Reichstag.

The essential flaw in this view was the failure to see that the western powers has reached their limit in 1939. Hitler was right to judge that Poland was not in itself of much intrinsic interest in British and French calculations, but he failed to see that both powers assessed the Polish crisis not on its own merits, but in terms of their global interests and great-power status. To fight for Poland was a means to assert British and French power in the Balkans, the Mediterranean and the Far East as well. Given favourable Allied intelligence on the military balance, and the threat of severe economic crisis if war preparations were continued at such a high level into the future, the Polish crisis was viewed as an unrepeatable opportunity to challenge German expansion. If war had to come – and the Allies hoped fervently that Hitler would see reason before it did – the late summer of 1939 was a good time to declare it. This was particularly so given the nature of the Allied strategy of blockade and economic warfare, which could be made to bite across the winter months when Hitler would be unable to mount a major land offensive. The only incalculable element was the possibility of German bomb attacks in an effort to achieve the 'knock-out blow' dreamed of by air theorists. Great efforts were made over the summer to complete the necessary civil defence preparations, to arrange the evacuation of women and children, and to prepare for gas attack.

Why did Hitler fail to grasp the Allies' determination in 1939 to contain him? The first reason was the poor intelligence he received on Allied military preparations, which greatly underestimated Allied military strength and economic potential. Though Hitler knew that German preparations for a major war were far from complete, the evidence he was given suggested that British and French rearmament was still far behind German. He was fed, too, on a regular diet of ill-informed and selective information about the morale and political stability of the democracies [**Doc. 28, p. 122**]. He argued that if he called their bluff over Poland, they would be forced to stand back and would be plunged into political crisis. On the day after the signing of the German-Soviet Pact he called for copies of British and French newspapers so that he could read the news for himself of the collapse of Chamberlain and Daladier's governments. There was no such news. But as late as 31 August, the eve of the German attack on Poland, Goebbels recorded in his diary that 'the Führer does not believe England will intervene'.

This was not an entirely unrealistic view. Communications between the western powers and Poland were regularly intercepted by German intelligence organizations. French secret codes for diplomatic communication were easily read (Porch, 1993). The intercepted traffic showed that great pressure was being put on the Poles to make reasonable concessions to Berlin over the question of Danzig. German sources knew that Polish requests for arms and money were turned down by the west, and Hitler interpreted this at face value, further evidence that Britain and France were not serious (Prazmowska, 1987). All of this was resonant of the Czech crisis the year before. The British Ambassador, **Nevile Henderson**, gave the impression that the last thing Britain wanted was war, and that it was Polish, as much as German, intransigence that was the stumbling block. 'I have held from the beginning,' he wrote to London, 'that the Poles were utterly foolish and unwise' (HMSO, 1946–82: vol. 7, 198). German discussions with a number of British officials, politicians and businessmen during the summer of 1939 seemed to confirm the picture that Britain would have its price for Poland as it had had for Czechoslovakia [**Doc. 29, p. 123**]. In France there were bitter divisions between the Foreign Minister, Georges Bonnet, who led a group in favour of further negotiation, and Prime Minister Daladier, who wanted no further concessions to Germany [**Doc. 30, p. 123**]. But even Daladier told his cabinet on 24 August that the Poles 'must sacrifice Danzig. They ought to have done so earlier' (Adamthwaite, 1977: 222). Hitler's assessment of western will was based on a justified realism laced with a strong dose of wishful thinking.

There was no shortage of illusion in the west either. The stream of information from Berlin, though conflicting, seemed to suggest that Germany was facing severe crisis at home and that the possibility could not be excluded that the German government might be overthrown rather than face war with the west. Chamberlain hoped to the very last that Hitler would be reasonable and would come to terms rather than risk a war he could not win. The prospect of agreement was brought suddenly closer in the last week of August when Goering, apparently on his own initiative but with Hitler's backing, began to talk with the British government through a Swedish intermediary, **Birger Dahlerus**. The talks showed, however, that even the so-called moderates in Germany were not prepared to accept the major condition for any settlement with Poland, that Germany must show itself willing to work within a political framework acceptable to the western powers; in other words that Germany should reverse its policy of expansion in eastern Europe.

In the middle stood Poland. The Polish government would make no substantial concession to the German position on Danzig or the Polish Corridor [**Doc. 31, p. 124**]. The British and French put pressure on Poland throughout the last weeks of August to make at least some gesture that would conciliate Germany and bring it more readily to the conference table. But the Poles could see that they were faced now with a difficult choice. They could give way to German demands and end up as the Czechs had done, swallowed up piecemeal by the Reich; or they could remain firm in their defence of Polish sovereignty and face the prospect of fighting Germany. In the end they chose the latter, clinging to the Anglo-French guarantee for want of any alternative, but all too aware of what the likely outcome would be.

Henderson, Nevile (1882–1942): British diplomat who became Ambassador to Berlin in 1937. He was widely regarded as being a pro-German appeaser, a reputation that has recently been reassessed. He delivered the British ultimatum to the German government on 3 September 1939.

Dahlerus, Birger (1891–1957): Swedish businessman and a friend of Hermann Göring who acted unsuccessfully as an intermediary between Germany and Britain in the days before the outbreak of the Second World War.

These three elements, German illusions of western irresolution, British and French fears for their status as great powers, and Polish firmness, came together with explosive force in the last week of August 1939. Hitler postponed the invasion of Poland from 26 August until 31 August on hearing of the British-Polish treaty, and instructed Goering to increase his efforts to detach Britain from France. A flurry of diplomatic activity followed, in which the British sought to buy time by encouraging the Poles to send a negotiator to Berlin, as the Germans wanted, so that one last effort could be made to get Hitler to accept British and French terms. Hitler interpreted these efforts as final evidence of the irresolution and timidity of the west. 'Our enemies,' he announced some days before, 'have men who are below average. No personalities. No masters, men of action' (International Military Tribunal, 1947: vol. 3, 585). Though there remained an element of risk, as there had been in every move since the occupation of the Rhineland, Hitler now thought it much reduced by the pact with Stalin and his hazy information on the political morale of the west. Poland was given an ultimatum which amounted to accepting German domination. Warsaw refused to comply with the demand to send a plenipotentiary to negotiate terms in Berlin. On the morning of 1 September German troops invaded Poland.

The day before, Mussolini, convinced by his advisers of Italian military weakness, made one last effort to avert a general war, in case Italy should be forced willy-nilly into the conflict. On 31 August he proposed a conference of the powers to resolve the outstanding issues of the Versailles Settlement, including Poland. In France Bonnet reacted enthusiastically and Britain showed interest, but both powers insisted that a condition for such a conference was the withdrawal of German troops now on Polish soil. Count Ciano, the Italian Foreign Minister, could not bring himself to tell this to Hitler, and the idea of a conference collapsed [**Doc. 32, p. 125**]. Hitler saw in the west's delay in supporting Poland confirmation that the Allies were trying to extricate themselves from their promise as he had expected, and ignored the British and French ultimata demanding an end to hostilities. After two days of final preparations for evacuation and mobilization which led to an unnecessary delay in presenting British and French demands (and infuriated the British parliament) Britain declared war on Germany at 11 a.m. on 3 September, with Chamberlain still hoping that Hitler might thus be deterred from taking further action [**Doc. 33, p. 125**].

Daladier had received a letter from Berlin on 31 August insisting that Hitler was on his knees and would back down if the west held firm (Reynaud, 1955). Buoyed up with this information, but with grave misgivings, he announced to the French Chamber of Deputies that France was at war from 5 p.m. on 3 September: 'In honouring our word we fight to defend our soil, our homes, our liberties' (Ministry of Foreign Affairs, 1940).

Though neither power entered the war without a sense of profound unease, there was none of the panic and uncertainty of August 1914, nor the enthusiasm. The prospect of war had been accepted months before, and repeatedly confirmed in the days leading up to the German invasion. Faced with a general war, Italy remained neutral, on the grounds that Germany would not provide it with the economic resources necessary for it to intervene effectively. There was consternation in Berlin that the west had called Hitler's bluff. Goering angrily telephoned Ribbentrop: 'Now you have your damned war.'

6

From European to World War

It is possible to argue that the war that broke out in 1939 was not simply a limited European war but a world war. The French and British Empires rallied to support the home countries. Economic warfare was carried on against Germany across the world. The entry of Italy into the war in the summer of 1940 spread the physical area of conflict to Africa and the Middle East. Yet until 1941 the war was essentially about the domination of the European continent by the European great powers. Not until Germany attacked the Soviet Union in June 1941 and the Japanese attacked the United States in December of the same year did the war assume world proportions and become, as Hitler had perhaps always intended, a real contest for world power.

THE WAR IN THE WEST

For the western powers the war against Hitler proved to be disastrous. The strategic calculations which encouraged them to stand firm in September 1939 were exposed as fatally flawed. The rapid defeat of Poland was not unexpected, as both the western powers had always recognized the military impossibility of doing anything in the short term to save Poland. For six months they conducted the war – the so-called 'Phoney War' – more or less along the lines they had hoped for. Both sides continued to undertake secret negotiations and soundings to see if agreement could be reached. Many Germans expected the Allies to abandon the war once Poland was beyond help, divided between Germany and Russia according to the terms of a second German-Soviet accord, signed on 28 September. In October Hitler announced proposals for peace before the German Reichstag [**Doc. 34, p. 126**]. But neither side was willing to begin negotiations except on their own terms, a prospect that could not be entertained by either Germany or the Allies. Chamberlain clung to the hope that Germany would still be

Phoney War: The period between September 1939 and May 1940 when there was very little military activity between Germany, Britain and France.

deterred by the sight of British and French military and economic strength. In October he told Roosevelt that Britain would not win 'by a complete and spectacular victory, but by convincing the Germans that they cannot win' (Offner, 1975: 165).

This was to be done, as the Allies had planned, by blockade and economic warfare, and by using their political influence to isolate Germany. Favourable agreements on war trade were reached with Spain, Greece, Holland, Belgium and Scandinavia. The British and French navies immediately began their efforts to place Germany in economic quarantine. Plans were laid to attack Germany at what were supposed to be its economic weak spots, the supply of iron ore from Sweden and the supply of oil from Romania and the Caucasus. The plans for oil show the general drift of Allied strategic thinking. In January 1940 the French Prime Minister instructed the armed forces to draw up plans for attacking Soviet oil installations and for interrupting Black Sea shipping which supplied Hitler with vital raw materials. General Gamelin, French Commander-in-Chief, reported that the best method was to bomb the Caucasus oilfields and to stir up Muslim revolt against the Soviet government in southern Russia. In March Gamelin issued a statement to the effect that both oil and Swedish ore must be seized and cut off from Germany, with priority to be given to oil supplies, 'to make the economic stranglehold on Germany tighter' (Richardson, 1973: 142). But these were difficult schemes to put into practice, and preparations were interrupted when Germany invaded Norway in April (thus protecting the iron ore supplies in Sweden) then France on 10 May, which ended all thought by the Allies of immediate action against the Soviet Union.

In practice the blockade could not be operated effectively; and the Allies exaggerated the extent to which Germany's capacity or will for war would be affected in the short term by the loss of either Swedish iron ore or Soviet oil. Allied military preparations were confused and poorly co-ordinated. Belgium refused to allow Allied troops to move to the Belgian-German border as had been hoped, so that the Maginot Line became at once more vulnerable than the French had planned because it could be outflanked to the north. Although there was plenty of intelligence available on German plans to attack and on German strength, the assault when it came was devastating in its speed and competence. Despite an overall balance of material forces that favoured the western states (135 German divisions against 152 Allied, 2,439 German tanks against 4,204 Allied, 3,369 aircraft against 4,981) the Allies were defeated by the superior fighting skills and daring strategic planning of the German forces, factors that the Allies had failed to take sufficiently into account. Fundamental mistakes were also made on the Allied side – although the west enjoyed larger numbers of aircraft, a majority of them were kept away from the fighting front, allowing German air forces to gain local air superiority vital to the conduct of modern, mobile warfare. As French defeat became imminent, Britain abandoned full military support in Europe and withdrew what forces it could to the final defence of southern England. On 22 June 1940 France signed an armistice, and German domination of Europe became fact.

For Britain this was the worst possible outcome. It exposed the extent of wishful thinking on the Allies' side about the strategy of blockade and containment. French and British power on the Continent was broken, and Britain, not Germany, faced the prospect of diplomatic isolation, even of blockade. The extent and competence of the victory surprised even Hitler, who with his generals had been apprehensive about German chances in the campaign. As it turned out, German war preparations, though incomplete, had proved equal to a military contest with the western states. They reached their limit in the failure to defeat Britain from the air, or to launch an invasion of southern England in the autumn of 1940. German forces and equipment had not been built up to face the task of seaborne assault with much chance of success. But it nevertheless appeared that Britain was now weakened, perhaps fatally, as a great power. The German tone in the summer became more dictatorial. Britain was offered the prospect of peace on German terms (an offer which Chamberlain's successor as Prime Minister, **Winston Churchill**, refused to consider, though Halifax thought German terms ought to be examined first). Plans were laid in Berlin to reconstruct the colonial areas of Africa in Germany's favour. A **New Order** was declared in Europe. Germany began the task of co-ordinating the economic resources of the conquered areas into a single German-dominated economic bloc.

To make things worse, Germany's Axis partners used the opportunity provided by German successes to advance their own imperial ambitions. Italy joined the war shortly before the defeat of France and launched an attack directed towards the Suez Canal and Britain's vital interests in the Middle East. In the Far East Japan used the opportunity of the defeat of the Netherlands and France to put pressure on their colonial possessions in the Far East. In September 1940 Japanese troops were stationed in French Indo-China by agreement with the French authorities there. On 27 September 1940 the Axis powers signed a **Tripartite Pact** to provide mutual assistance in the reconstruction of the international system [**Doc. 35, p. 127**].

In the latter part of 1940 Britain's position was undermined even further by the onset of economic crisis much along the lines predicted in 1939. The American Ambassador in London reported that 'Britain is busted'. British officials urged on their American colleagues the need for greater American help, without which Britain would simply no longer be able to buy the raw materials, food and armaments needed to sustain the war. The American attitude to the conflict was from the outset to avoid any political or military

Churchill, Winston (1874–1965): English politician, soldier and writer. Chancellor of the Exchequer from 1926 to 1929, in the 1930s he was on the political fringes until 1939 when he took over the Admiralty. In May 1940 he became Prime Minister, a post that he held until 1945, and again from 1951 to 1955.

New Order: Term usually associated with fascist plans for a new social order or a new international order. The 'old' order was in both cases identified with the political system of the west and its traditional European empires.

Tripartite Pact: Agreement signed between Germany, Italy and Japan on 27 September 1940 dividing the world into spheres of influence between them. Hungary, Romania and Slovakia later affiliated to the Pact.

involvement, while demonstrating in its economic policy sympathy for the Allied cause. Like Wilson before him, Roosevelt dreamt of being able to bring peace in Europe by hosting a great congress of the powers. Until the German attack on France in May 1940 American leaders still thought that it might be possible to reach an agreement with Hitler if the Allies would modify their conditions for negotiations. Even after the defeat of France the United States refused to enter into any sort of undertaking which might be interpreted as a political commitment. The British were now much keener on American assistance. On 25 May the British Chiefs-of-Staff wrote that unless the United States gave 'full economic and financial support . . . *we do not think we could continue the war with any chance of success*' (Peden, 1984: 332).

For Roosevelt there were the usual domestic political considerations. Though the Neutrality Act had been modified in November 1939 to allow the Allies to obtain more supplies, new restrictions were imposed in June 1940 in order to safeguard American rearmament, which was finally set in motion in May of that year. 1940 was election year in the United States and Roosevelt was well aware that he could not afford to alienate the isolationist sectors of the electorate by making too many concessions to the British position. When concessions were made they were on the basis of conditions favourable to American interests, the eventuality that the British had feared in 1939. In August the British were given fifty destroyers in return for eight American naval and air bases on British colonial territory in the western hemisphere from Newfoundland to British Guiana. Increased credit for British purchases in America was granted only on the promise that Britain would liquidate all its remaining foreign assets as far as it could to pay for them, and would also transfer £42 million of gold reserves stored in South Africa. When the United States finally agreed to give Britain military equipment under a Lend-Lease agreement in February 1941, it was only on the understanding that Britain had finally exhausted all its ability to pay. Britain's continued capacity to prosecute the war now rested on American goodwill (Kimball, 1969).

BARBAROSSA

In the summer of 1940 Hitler ordered the German armed forces to build up a huge army of 180 divisions, with 20 motorized and armoured divisions at its core, for the purpose of turning east against the Soviet Union. So successful had German forces proved to be that Hitler was now convinced that he could have his great war, originally scheduled for the mid-1940s, in 1940 and 1941 instead. Defeat of the Soviet Union first also fitted in with the time-scale and nature of German armaments policy. Though large new production plans were laid down for the air force and navy, they would not be ready to fight the Anglo-Saxon powers effectively for at least another two years. Army equipment, on the other hand, was already very large, and was planned to expand further in 1941. Far from contemplating the limited use of economic resources, an argument first put forward in 1945 by the American postwar survey on the effects of bombing, Hitler ordered the large-scale conversion of the German economy for war from the autumn of 1939 [**Doc. 36, p. 128**]. The rate of increase of military spending rose fastest in 1940 and 1941. By the onset of the campaign against the Soviet Union the level of civilian consumption had fallen by 24 per cent in two years, against a fall of only 10 per cent in Britain (Overy, 1994b).

Hitler based his strategy on the assumption that Britain could safely be left in isolation to be defeated later once the Soviet Union had been destroyed. Defeat of the Soviet Union would free him from fear of a war on two fronts, and bring Britain to the negotiating table. It would also free Japan in the east to contain the United States and prevent American aid for Britain [**Doc. 37, p. 128**]. The Barbarossa campaign meant more than this, however. The Soviet Union was the promised land of German *Lebensraum*, living space. Conquest of the Soviet Union also opened up the promise of world power, and would give Germany access to vast economic resources which the Anglo-Saxon powers could not match. Defeat of the Soviet Union held out the prospect of a drive towards India and British interests in the Middle East. Hitler hinted at a final reckoning with the United States.

Operation Barbarossa: Code name given to the German invasion of the USSR. The directive for the operation was laid down by Hitler on 18 December 1940, and the invasion by 4 million German, Hungarian, Romanian and Finnish forces began on 22 June 1941.

Rommel, Field Marshal Erwin (1891–1944): German tank commander in the early stages of the Second World War. He was posted to head German forces in North Africa in 1941, but was defeated by British Commonwealth forces at El Alamein. He was implicated in the July Plot to murder Hitler in 1944 and committed suicide.

On 18 December the German armed forces were issued with instructions for the attack on the Soviet Union, code-named **Operation Barbarossa** [**Doc. 38, p. 129**]. It was to be carried out in the late spring and summer of 1941. As it turned out, the plan's fantastic nature was compromised by events. British success in defeating Italian forces in Africa compelled Hitler to intervene on Italy's behalf by sending a small expeditionary force under **General Rommel**. In the Balkans Italy had launched an attack on Greece in October 1940 but was facing defeat there as well. In late March a *coup d'état* was staged in Yugoslavia against the pro-German regime in Belgrade, and on 6 April Hitler ordered an attack on Yugoslavia, followed by a short campaign to defeat the Greek army and rescue his Italian ally, both completed by the end of the month. As a result of the move to the Balkans the attack on the Soviet Union was postponed from May to late June, which meant that German forces had much less time than expected before the onset of the autumn rains in Russia, and the tough Russian winter. It was also found in the spring that German military production had been much less successful than expected, largely due to the high levels of military interference in the planning and development of arms production. The factor weighing most strongly in the Germans' favour was the element of surprise. Despite numerous warnings from a wide number of intelligence sources, all of which pointed towards an imminent German invasion, and some of which revealed the exact date, Stalin obstinately refused to accept that the warnings were anything more than British-inspired provocations designed to lure the Soviet Union into a war with Germany in order to ease the pressure on the embattled British Empire. He could see no rationality or justification for German invasion. Soviet supplies were punctually sent under the terms of trade agreements, the last of which had been signed in January 1941 (indeed trains loaded with Soviet supplies were still rolling across the frontier the day Germany attacked). Germany was facing a powerful enemy in the west and was now involved in southern Europe and the Mediterranean; Stalin could not believe that Hitler would attack a state as militarily strong as the Soviet Union with his other war unresolved. At the last moment, under growing pressure from his commanders who could see the reality more clearly than Stalin, he ordered troops on the frontier to alert, but the orders arrived as Axis forces poured across the border. The element of surprise was almost complete on the morning of 22 June.

The German invasion of the Soviet Union ended the anxieties felt in London and Washington about the possibility of a German-Soviet alliance to overthrow the existing world order. Soviet policy in eastern Europe from September 1939 had lent weight to these fears. Soviet forces occupied eastern Poland on 17 September, and a second German-Soviet agreement on 28 September confirmed the Polish partition. Between 25 September and 10 October 1939 the Baltic states, Estonia, Latvia and Lithuania, were pressured to accept Soviet troops on their soil, and became in effect Soviet protectorates. In November 1939 the Soviet Union attacked Finland, after the Finnish government rejected demands for territorial concessions and Soviet bases on Finnish soil. After a brief but inglorious campaign, in which the Red Army suffered 100,000 casualties, the Finns agreed to Soviet demands in March 1940. In June, while Germany was fully occupied in the west, Stalin seized the opportunity to incorporate the remaining areas assigned to the Soviet sphere of influence under the German-Soviet agreements. The Baltic states were fully integrated into the Soviet Union, and Romania was forced to concede the territories of Bessarabia and the northern Bukovina, which had been taken from Russia in 1918. The Soviet Union put further pressure on the states of south-eastern Europe, and in November 1940, when Soviet Foreign Minister Molotov visited Berlin, asked German leaders for a further agreement which would give the Soviet Union control of the Dardenelles Straits leading from the Black Sea, and would turn Bulgaria into a virtual Soviet dependency [**Doc. 39, p. 129**].

Some historians have seen in all this a coherent Soviet plan to take over eastern Europe and to expand the communist empire westward into the rest of the continent. It was true that Stalin believed that the war might create conditions, as the First World War had done, for popular revolutions across Europe against the capitalist order. But there is no evidence that there existed any coherent plan. Stalin expanded Soviet interests in eastern Europe opportunistically, as Hitler had done before 1939. His priority was security against any threat posed to him by the other major powers (Roberts, 1995). The Soviet Union was not yet prepared to fight a major war. However, the effect of Soviet moves in eastern Europe was to confirm for Hitler the wisdom of his decision to launch war against Stalin before the Soviet position was strengthened any further. Soviet efforts to improve security in eastern Europe in fact made war against the Soviet Union more likely.

The invasion of the Soviet Union brought relief to Britain militarily. It was now possible for Britain to pursue a peripheral strategy in Africa and the Middle East, while building up large air defence forces at home and a bomber fleet to attack the German war economy. But the attack still left unresolved America's position in the conflict. The most the British could extract was a promise from Roosevelt in December 1940 that the United States would be 'the arsenal of democracy', and pledges in the **Atlantic Charter** drawn up in August 1941 by Churchill and Roosevelt to introduce self-determination and free trade in Europe if Britain should win. In the background American trade officials continued to work, as they had done since 1938, to undo Britain's commitment to imperial preference, a concession that Britain was finally compelled to make in February 1942. Roosevelt remained worried throughout 1941 about the effects of a military commitment on domestic opinion until it was certain that America's vital political interests were at stake. **Morgenthau**, the Treasury Secretary, argued for war in May. Roosevelt's reply was 'I am waiting to be pushed into this' (Offner, 1975: 204). The German-Soviet war opened up new uncertainties. Some American leaders believed that the Soviet Union would be quickly defeated, a fact that America could do little to prevent, but which would profoundly alter the balance of power against it. Others, Roosevelt included, thought that the Soviet Union would resist Hitler and perhaps make American intervention in Europe unnecessary. British blockade and bombing could be expected to do the rest. Like Chamberlain before 1939, Roosevelt prepared for war while hoping that it could at all costs be avoided or fought for him by others (Heinrichs, 1988).

Atlantic Charter: Declaration prepared by Churchill and Roosevelt at their meeting in Placentia Bay, Newfoundland, 9–12 August 1941. The Charter was a commitment to promoting the self-determination of peoples and democratic institutions.

Morgenthau, Henry (1891–1967): American Democrat politician who became Treasury Secretary in the Roosevelt government from 1934 to 1945. He is best remembered for his 'plan' to turn Germany into an agrarian state after the war as a punishment.

THE COMING OF WORLD WAR

The United States was also deeply concerned about developments in the Far East. For many Americans the Pacific was a more important sphere of interest than Europe because the Japanese Empire posed a greater immediate threat to United States' interests than did Germany. Since the outbreak of the European war, conditions in the Far East had continued to deteriorate for the western powers. Japan began a cautious move southwards against the poorly defended colonial empires. In September the French administration in Indo-China was forced to accept an effective Japanese protectorate. Thailand was compelled to offer Japan military bases and to become a virtual dependency. Japan now dominated the South China Sea, threatening Malaya, the Dutch East Indies and the Philippines, where there were American military bases. Some Japanese politicians opposed further expansion, for fear of driving the United States to war. But the military and their civilian political allies argued that Japan was still far from self-sufficient in vital raw materials and could not defend its empire successfully until these had been guaranteed. Further expansion was a necessary condition for retaining what had already been won. This argument became more pressing in July 1940 when the United States began a partial embargo on the export of iron and oil to Japan. Japanese leaders feared that an economic encirclement might be imposed on Japan before the new economic resources could be captured. During 1941 Japan's financial position deteriorated sharply and by the summer it had nearly exhausted its foreign exchange reserves, which were necessary to fund the imports of strategic raw materials. At the same time arguments about foreign policy led the armed forces to impose authoritarian rule on Japan under the so-called 'New Structure' of government. Domestic political conflict and economic crisis pushed Japan towards a policy of renewed expansion and a confrontation with the other Pacific powers (Butow, 1961).

The situation in Europe encouraged the Japanese military to seize an opportunity that might not present itself again. France was defeated and could do nothing to save its empire in the east. Britain, it was believed, was close to defeat, which would leave the United States with the possibility of a two-ocean war for which it was not militarily prepared. The only problem was the position of the Soviet Union. In April 1941 the Japanese signed a non-aggression pact in Moscow which brought temporary security to the north. The German attack on the Soviet Union in June made it improbable that the Soviet Union would do anything to prevent Japan from moving southwards. There was a growing belief that neither Britain nor the United States would be able or willing to resist further Japanese aggression, a calculation not very different from Hitler's in 1939 and, as it turned out, just as wrong. Once achieved, the southern empire would be a basis for negotiating with the west from a position of strength.

The British position in the Far East was militarily untenable. Britain, as a result, avoided doing anything that might incite the Japanese. The British even argued for giving Japan a free hand in China if that would divert Japan for the time being away from the British Empire. The United States, while objecting to such a blatant appeasement of Japan, nevertheless sought throughout 1940 and 1941 to find grounds for full negotiations with the Japanese on terms acceptable to both sides. It was hoped that the Japanese 'moderates' would be encouraged by signs of American willingness to talk, to persuade the military to abandon expansion in favour of conciliation. This proved as empty a strategy as it had done with the German moderates, for not even the more conciliatory Japanese leaders were prepared at the time to consider forgoing any of the gains they had already made. Though unofficial American and Japanese negotiators drew up a Draft Agreement in April 1941 as a preliminary to formal talks, the Japanese would not undertake to end their aggression in China and the United States would not accept the 1938 New Order declaration as a starting-point for discussion. Nevertheless, America did not close the door on negotiation, a fact which the Japanese took as evidence that the United States was still very uncertain about risking war at all (Divine, 1965).

United States strategy in the Far East was faced by a number of difficulties. Rearmament on any scale was initiated only in 1940. Priority was given to the defence of the American mainland. A slow trickle of forces and equipment moved out to American bases in the Far East. By December 1941 there were still only thirty-five modern bombers in the Philippines instead of the one hundred promised. There were domestic political problems to contend with too. Conscription was approved in Congress by only 203 votes to 202, evidence of the still widespread support for isolationism. There was pressure from within governing circles not to take any action which might be construed by the public as helping to preserve the British colonial empire, although Roosevelt and his military advisers were not in favour of a strategy which was directed only at Japan and which abandoned Britain. 'Our strategy of self-defence,' wrote Roosevelt to the American Ambassador in Tokyo, 'must be a global strategy' (Offner, 1975: 193). The military chiefs wanted a strategy if war came of 'Europe first', while a defensive line was held in the Pacific. But in public the impression had to be given that the government was not about to plunge into a European conflict while there existed a visible threat to American territory in the west. This dilemma led to a certain paralysis in American policy in the second half of 1941, which was detected by Japanese leaders as they assessed the right time to strike.

On 2 July 1941 the Japanese cabinet, dominated by its military members, decided to complete the programme for the establishment of an Asian New Order, whatever the American reaction might be [Doc. 40, p. 130]. Indo-China was formally annexed. Military preparations for a possible war with the United States, which had begun in January, were now directed towards attacks on American positions in Hawaii and the Philippines, and on the British naval base at Singapore, the centrepiece of Britain's Far Eastern defences. There was no unanimity on this strategy, for there were generals and politicians who still preferred a northern campaign against the Soviet Union. The German attack made this a more feasible option. In August Ribbentrop tried to persuade the Japanese Ambassador that Japan should help to finish off the stumbling Soviet state before turning south [**Doc. 41, p. 130**]. The Japanese Foreign Minister, Matsuoko, added his voice to the argument in favour of exploiting German victory by extending the Japanese Empire deep into Soviet Asia. The southern strategy prevailed only because the conquest of the rich raw material and oil resources of south-east Asia was regarded as the vital prerequisite for any further extension of the Japanese Empire.

In October 1941 the new Prime Minister, **General Hideki Tojo**, put Japanese demands to the United States for a free hand in Asia. It was agreed in secret that if America should refuse, which was likely, war would be started by 8 December. The oil situation for Japan was now critical. Admiral Yamamoto, Commander of the Japanese navy, doubted whether Japan could prosecute any war successfully unless it were declared as soon as possible. To make certain of capturing the so-called 'southern region', and of holding a defensive perimeter around the new empire, the Japanese navy trained large numbers of specialist air crews in dive-bomb and torpedo attack, who would be used to inflict crippling damage on American and British naval power. Japanese intelligence confirmed how poorly defended American and British positions were. German information suggested that the Soviet Union was on the point of defeat and Hitler now hinted at help for the Japanese if they attacked the United States. The Japanese Emperor, **Hirohito**, was informed that Japan's future as a great power was at stake if the favourable opportunity to strike was not taken. 'If there were no war,' the Chief of the Naval Staff Nagano told the Emperor, 'the fate of the nation was sealed. Even if there is war, the country may be ruined. Nevertheless a nation which does not fight in this plight has lost its spirit and is already a doomed nation' (Dull, 1978: 5). On 29 November the final order was given for war. On 7 December Japanese aircraft attacked the American naval base at Pearl Harbor in Hawaii.

Four days later Hitler declared war on the United States. Roosevelt was thus released from the responsibility of taking his country into war against the wishes of large numbers of Americans, and ostensibly in the interests of the British Empire or Soviet communism. German and Japanese action now threatened America's vital interests. There was no doubting in Washington that the war should be prosecuted with all the power at America's disposal.

Why did Hitler declare war on the United States when his other major enemies were still undefeated? There is much to be said for the case that Hitler had always intended at some stage to face the United States in a contest for world power, if Germany was successful in dominating Europe and defeating Russia. His attitude to America was coloured by the same

Tojo, General Hideki (1884–1948): Japanese soldier and politician who became Minister of War in July 1940 and then Prime Minister in October 1941, shortly before the Japanese attack on Pearl Harbor. He resigned in July 1944, following Japanese defeats, and was tried and executed as a war criminal in 1948.

Hirohito, Emperor of Japan (1901–89): The last traditional emperor of Japan, he oversaw Japanese expansion in the 1930s and agreed to the war with the United States in 1941. In 1945 he announced Japanese surrender but remained in office as a constitutional head of state.

self-deluding racialism that characterized all his foreign policy. America for Hitler was a decadent power, vitiated by poorer racial elements, blacks and Jews. Hitler and Goering were dismissive of American military power. American pacifism and isolationism were taken as evidence of fundamental weaknesses (Weinberg, 1981). German military intelligence attempted to alert Hitler to the real economic strength of the United States, but its reports were deliberately suppressed. No doubt Hitler was also influenced by what he thought was the imminent defeat of the Soviet Union, which would release vast economic resources for use against the United States. Instructions had been sent out to the arms industry months before to give priority after the defeat of the Soviet Union to an enormous increase in naval and aerial strength to be turned against the Anglo-Saxon powers. Though there was a wilful lack of realism in his reasoning, it is easy to see how Hitler, with his forces at the edge of Moscow and pushing towards Egypt, and with news of the destruction of the American Pacific fleet, must have felt that he held in his hand the prospect of German world power.

There were, however, more mundane considerations. From a German point of view the United States had been close to belligerency for over a year. Economic warfare was already being conducted against Germany. Lend-Lease provided a stream of munitions and resources for Germany's enemies. In the Battle of the Atlantic America had been compelled, through German attacks on American shipping, to take a more active role. American troops and aircraft were stationed in Greenland and Iceland. Hitler could not see, as the British could, the strains in the Anglo-American relationship, and he interpreted the Atlantic Charter as a deliberate provocation inspired by western Jews in the face of German efforts to build the European New Order. By December 1941 there seemed a strong possibility that the United States would declare war formally on Germany. Ribbentrop told his State Secretary at the Foreign Ministry that great powers did not wait to have war declared upon them.

The underlying irony was that the German declaration of war brought into the conflict the one state which in 1941 was capable of undermining the position that Germany already occupied. The entry into war of the United States filled that power vacuum in world affairs which the Axis powers had been tempted to occupy from 1939 by the use of force. When the war ended almost four years later America and the Soviet Union, not Germany, were the world's major powers.

Part 3

ASSESSMENT

7

Hitler's War?

Wars are the outcome of a lack of stability, real or perceived, in the conduct of relations between states. They have causes of a general kind which form the context in which decisions about a specific conflict are taken. These general causes are in this sense permissive factors, without which the conditions will not arise for a particular war. The cause of the Second World War was not just Hitler. The war was brought about by the interplay between specific factors, of which Hitler was one, and the more general causes making for instability in the international system.

These general causes can be traced back, as we have seen, to the strains placed on the diplomatic world in the late nineteenth century by the rise of nationalism, empire-building and industrial power. The First World War was fought to resolve these tensions but failed to do so. The major victors, Britain and France, rearranged Europe at the end of the war in an effort to re-establish equilibrium in world affairs. Having done so they became committed, with some minor qualifications, to the *status quo*. Weakened by the war, and declining relatively in economic strength, both powers were faced by a galaxy of states and political forces opposed, for one reason or another, to the *status quo*. These included not only the defeated powers, but also Japan in the Far East, Italy in the Mediterranean and, of greater significance, both Russia and the United States. Stalin explained this to the British Ambassador in 1940: 'The USSR had wanted to change the old equilibrium . . . but England and France had wanted to preserve it' (Weinberg, 1981: 7). In America the postwar settlement was regarded as a victory for old-fashioned imperialism. Though they expressed their opinions less bluntly than Stalin, American statesmen shared the same loose assumption about altering the equilibrium by undermining colonialism and reorganizing the world economic system.

In assessing the causes of the war we might well ask why the Soviet Union and the United States did not impose their own idea of equilibrium at a stage earlier than 1945. The answer lies partly in the fact that until the world depression it was not entirely clear that Britain and France, in co-operation with other League powers, could not make the Versailles system work. Both were regarded, rightly or wrongly, as the 'super-powers' of their day. But the explanation lies principally in the fact that for compelling reasons in domestic politics neither the Soviet Union nor the United States was in a position to exert its influence with any profound effect in world affairs. American **isolationism** and, after 1935, open neutrality, and the need to consolidate communist power inside Russia, held both states back from major intervention in international politics. Nor, it should be added, was Europe prepared to abandon its traditional position at the centre of the world stage. Europe possessed a wealth of diplomatic experience, commercial strength and political influence. Its moral ascendancy was taken for granted.

Isolationism: The popular American view in the 1920s and 1930s that the United States should avoid any foreign political or military commitments.

In practice European influence, and in particular that of Britain and France, was in decline. After 1932 the postwar settlement began to break down. Incoherently and uncertainly at first, a reordering was set in motion. It was spurred on by economic crisis and the deep resentments and hostility engendered by 'beggar my neighbour' policies. Great importance must be attached to the changing 'mentality' of international conduct in the 1930s. Fixed points in the system gradually gave way, giving the widespread appearance of dissolution and collapse and reviving fears of general war. From 1935 onwards war of some kind, civil war or invasion, was being fought in one or other part of the world. As the international system relapsed into increasing chaos there inevitably emerged at certain points specific ambitions to take advantage of the crisis. In Germany, Japan and Italy were political forces strongly influenced by social-Darwinist, nationalist ideology, which stood to gain by any change in the international distribution of power. All these movements expressed a clear commitment to expansion and war to achieve what they wanted. But all three states remained trapped in the framework imposed by the major imperial powers. It was assumed in each country, and not simply by its leaders, that colonies, empire-building, the scramble for possession of economic spoils, were all perennial features of the world system. Domestic nationalism was translated into conventional demands for empire and spheres of influence.

As the weaknesses of the system were exposed, those states with plans for readjustment were tempted to go further. The isolation of America and the Soviet Union, with their tacit acceptance of changes in the *status quo*, provided further encouragement. Britain and France were both forced to decide whether or not to contest this challenge, and under what circumstances. Very little could be done without rearmament, but there was a certain flexibility in the system which allowed concessions to be made to all three aggressor states within terms acceptable to British and French interests. Active confrontation was postponed for as long as possible to allow their military strength to build up and to avoid domestic crisis at home, and also because it was not then apparent, as it is now to historians, what the ambitions of the three powers were. For much of the time Soviet Russia was distrusted as much as Germany. Neither Britain nor France wished to weaken Europe to the extent that the USSR might benefit.

Only when it became clear that Germany posed a real threat to British and French interests and could no longer be accommodated without destroying their status as great powers did they decide with grave misgivings that war was necessary. Economic and military preparations, which provoked growing domestic crisis, pointed to the desirability of confronting Germany in 1939 by denying Hitler the free hand in eastern Europe which he thought he had won at Munich. Of course if Hitler had not decided to solve his 'Polish problem' in 1939, in the expectation that the Allies would now back down and accept the shift in the balance of power, the western powers would not have fought in September 1939. But they could now clearly see the implications for them of Hitler's appetite for expansion. Even Chamberlain accepted that Hitler was beyond appeasing. On 5 September 1939 he wrote to the Archbishop of Canterbury: 'I did so hope that we were going to escape these tragedies. But I sincerely believe that with that madman it was impossible' (Catterall and Morris, 1993: 5). At some point in 1939 or 1940 Britain and France were determined to confront him and enforce limits on German action, and had popular support at home to do so. Had everything gone according to plan and had Germany either backed down or been defeated by blockade and bombing, a not entirely unrealistic hope in 1939, Chamberlain might have achieved his grand settlement after all. It should not be forgotten that Britain and France went to war in 1939 in the expectation that this would be the outcome: that Germany could be defeated by the western powers on their own.

Could the war have been prevented? It is sometimes argued that it was feeble statesmanship that brought about war. Had Britain and France been prepared to confront the dictators sooner, even to the extent of fighting for the Rhineland in 1936 or the Sudetenland in 1938, then major war would never have been necessary. This is to ignore the reality confronting British and French leaders in the 1930s. They were faced with a confusion of different pressures both at home and abroad which at times must have appeared quite beyond the ability of even the most gifted statesman to resolve. As it was, they chose to find areas for compromise which did not fatally weaken British and French interests, as they saw them, while retaining political stability at home and the survival of their economic systems. It is wishful thinking to suppose, even if such things had been politically possible, that a display of strength in March 1936 by the western powers, or a higher level of arms spending in 1936 and 1937, would have very much reduced these pressures. It was not a lack of statesmanship that was at fault, but the basic weakness of the international structure which Britain and France were trying to salvage.

It has also been argued that the western powers misjudged the Polish crisis, that they should have allowed Hitler a free hand in eastern Europe, which would have brought him sooner or later into conflict with the Soviet Union, while throwing themselves on the mercy of the United States to restore stability in Europe and the Far East. This was, after all, what effectively happened between 1939 and 1941. But it ignores one crucial factor. Britain and France were determined to defend their status as great powers without resorting to dependence on either Russia or America. 'Pray God,' wrote Cadogan, 'we shall never have to depend on the Soviet or the United States' (Dilks, 1971). Theirs was an historic role, which could not be lightly abandoned. For so long the arbiters of world events, wealthy possessors of large empires, they both had a responsibility, a moral imperative, that required them to choose war rather than dishonour. If this seems a strangely archaic justification, it should be remembered, certainly in Britain's case, that much of the ruling class which dominated politics in the 1930s was infected with a sentimental and uncritical acceptance of Britain's role in the world derived from the heyday of Victorian imperial grandeur and 'civilizing' responsibility. This ruling class arrogated to themselves the role of judging the national interest. Rather than face the reality of declining power, which had caused the crisis in the first place, they chose a strategy of deterrence and containment, and finally war itself.

Only the active and powerful intervention of the Soviet Union and the United States might have averted war in 1939. But instead, as the crisis deepened, Stalin began the years of purges and political upheaval which neutralized the Red Army in the eyes of Germany and Japan; and Roosevelt bowed to domestic pressure for neutrality. Both stood back in 1939, alive to the fact that some sort of revision of the international system was now inevitable, but both anxious to avoid war as long as possible. After 1939 the international system became increasingly fluid. Germany, Italy and Japan concerted their efforts to replace Anglo-French power after June 1940 by a solid structure of their own which neither the Soviet Union nor America could undermine. In the end, however, it became apparent first to Hitler, then to the Japanese military, that this new equilibrium could not be established without the military defeat of the Soviet Union and the United States, which meant world war. Once embarked upon their own imperialism, they were forced to accept what Britain and France had been reluctant to accept in 1939: that no defence or revision of the *status quo* was possible without involving Soviet and American interests, whether in eastern Europe, China or the Middle East. Hitler's invasion of the Soviet Union, and Japan's attack on the United

States were gambles for the highest stakes, the chance to achieve world power status at a critical point of transition in the international system.

It did not automatically follow that the final involvement of the USSR and America in the war would bring to an end the brief two years of Axis ascendancy. But any realistic assessment of the strength of the two sides – and Britain's war effort was far from negligible – must conclude that as long as the Allies co-ordinated their activities and learned to fight effectively (neither of which was an inevitable outcome), a relative stability would be restored to the international system. This stability was based between 1945 and 1989 upon the balance of perceived strength between the United States and the Soviet Union, successors to the European 'great powers' system which collapsed after 1940.

Part 4

DOCUMENTS

Document 1   THE TREATY OF VERSAILLES AND GERMANY

Part IV. German rights and interests outside Germany

Article 118. In territory outside her European frontiers as fixed by the present Treaty, Germany renounces all rights, titles and privileges whatever in or over territory which belonged to her or her allies, and all rights, titles and privileges whatever their origin which she held as against the Allied and Associated Powers . . .

Section I. German colonies

Article 119. Germany renounces in favour of the Principal Allied and Associated Powers all her rights and titles over her overseas possessions . . .

Part V. Military, naval and air clauses

In order to render possible the initiation of a general limitation on armaments of all nations, Germany undertakes strictly to observe the military, naval and air clauses which follow.

Section I. Military clauses

Chapter I: Effectives and cadres of the German army.
Article 159. The German military forces shall be demobilized and reduced as prescribed hereinafter.

Article 160. By a date which must not be later than March 31, 1920, the German army must not comprise more than seven divisions of infantry and three divisions of cavalry.

   After that date the total number of effectives in the army of the States constituting Germany must not exceed one hundred thousand men, including officers and establishments of depots. The army shall be devoted exclusively to the maintenance of order within the territory and to the control of the frontiers . . .

Part VIII. Reparation

Section I. General Provisions

Article 231 [the 'war guilt' clause]. The Allied and Associated Governments affirm and Germany accepts the responsibility of Germany and her allies for causing all the loss and damage to which the Allied and Associated Governments and their nationals have been subjected as a consequence of the war imposed upon them by the aggression of Germany and her allies . . .
Article 233. The amount of the above damage for which compensation is to be made by Germany shall be determined by an Inter-Allied Commission, to be called the Reparation Commission . . .

Source: Extract from the Treaty of Peace between the Allied and Associated Powers and Germany, 28 June 1919 in Grenville (1974: 67–9).

THE COVENANT OF THE LEAGUE   **Document 2**

The High Contracting Parties,
In order to promote international co-operation and to achieve international peace and security

> by the acceptance of obligations not to resort to war, by the prescription of open, just and honourable relations between nations,
> by the firm establishment of the understandings of international law as the actual rule of conduct among Governments, and by the maintenance of justice and a scrupulous respect for all treaty obligations in the dealings of organized peoples with one another,

Agree to this Covenant of the League of Nations . . .

Article 8. The members of the League recognize that the maintenance of peace requires the reduction of national armaments to the lowest point consistent with national safety and the enforcement by common action of international obligations . . .
Article 10. The members of the League undertake to respect and preserve as against external aggression the territorial integrity and existing political independence of all members of the League . . .
Article 11. Any war or threat of war, whether immediately affecting any of the members of the League or not, is hereby declared a matter of concern to the whole League, and the League shall take any action that may be deemed wise and effectual to safeguard the peace of nations.

Source: Treaty of Versailles, 28 June 1919, Part I, the Covenant of the League of Nations, in Grenville (1974: 59–60).

THE SEARCH FOR A SETTLEMENT   **Document 3**

. . . the German visit was from my point of view a great success, because it achieved its object, that of creating an atmosphere in which it is possible to discuss with Germany the practical questions involved in a European settlement . . . Both Hitler and Goering said separately, and emphatically, that they had no desire or intention of making war, and I think we may take this as correct, at any rate for the present. Of course they want to dominate Eastern Europe; they want as close a union with Austria as they can get without incorporating her in the Reich, and they want much the same things for the Sudetendeutsche as we did for the Uitlanders in the Transvaal.

They want Togoland and Kameruns. I am not quite sure where they stand about S.W. Africa; but they do not insist on Tanganyika, if they can be given some reasonably equivalent territory on the West Coast, possibly to be carved out of Belgian Congo and Angola. I think they would be prepared to come back to the League, if it were shorn of its compulsory powers, now clearly shown to be ineffective, and though Hitler was rather non-committal about disarmament, he did declare himself in favour of the abolition of bombing aeroplanes.

Now here, it seems to me, is a fair basis of discussion, though no doubt all these points bristle with difficulties. But I don't see why we shouldn't say to Germany, 'give us satisfactory assurances that you won't use force to deal with the Austrians and Czechoslovakians, and we will give you similar assurances that we won't use force to prevent the changes you want, if you can get them by peaceful means'.

Source: Chamberlain memorandum, 26 November 1937, in Feiling (1946: 332–3).

Document 4   AMERICAN 'APPEASEMENT'

This country constantly and consistently advocates maintenance of peace. We advocate national and international self-restraint. We advocate abstinence by all nations from use of force in pursuit of policy and from interference in the internal affairs of other nations. We advocate adjustment of problems in international relations by processes of peaceful negotiation and agreement. We advocate faithful observance of international agreements. Upholding the principle of the sanctity of treaties, we believe in modification of provisions of treaties, when need therefore arises, by orderly processes carried out in a spirit of mutual helpfulness and accommodation.

Source: Statement by Secretary of State Cordell Hull, 16 July 1937, in US Department of State (1933–41: vol. 1, 1937, 700).

Document 5   STALIN ANTICIPATES WAR

One result of the protracted economic crisis has been the hitherto unprecedented tension in the political situation in capitalist countries, both within these countries and in their mutual relations. The intensified struggle for foreign markets, the disappearance of the last vestiges of free trade, prohibitive tariffs, trade war, currency war, dumping, and many other analogous measures which demonstrate extreme nationalism in economic policy have made the relations among the various countries extremely strained, have prepared the ground for military conflicts, and have put war on the order of the day as a means for a new redivision of the world and of spheres of influence in favour of the stronger States . . .

It is not surprising that bourgeois pacifism is now dragging out a miserable existence, and that idle talk of disarmament is giving way to 'businesslike' talk about armament and rearmament. Again, as in 1914, the parties of bellicose imperialism, the parties of war and revenge, are coming into the foreground. Quite clearly things are heading for a new war . . . Still others, again, think that war should be organised against the USSR. Their plan is to defeat the USSR, divide up its territory, and profit at its expense. It would be a mistake to believe that it is only certain military circles in Japan who think this way. We know that similar plans are being hatched in the leading political circles of certain European states.

Source: Report by Stalin to the 17th Congress of the CPSU, 26 January 1934, in Degras (1951–3: vol. 3, 65–8).

THE 'HOSSBACH MEMORANDUM'   **Document 6**

The Führer began by stating that the subject of the present conference was of such importance that its discussion would, in other countries, certainly be a matter for a full Cabinet meeting, but he – the Führer – had rejected the idea of making it a subject of discussion before the wider circle of the Reich Cabinet just because of the importance of the matter. His exposition to follow was the fruit of his $4^1/_2$ years in power. He wished to explain to the gentlemen present his basic ideas concerning the opportunities for the development of our position in the field of foreign affairs and its requirements, and he asked, in the interests of a long-term German policy, that his exposition be regarded, in the event of his death, as his last will and testament.

The Führer then continued:

The aim of German policy was to make secure and to preserve the racial community and to enlarge it. It was therefore a question of space.

The German racial community comprised over 85 million people and, because of their number and the narrow limits of habitable space in Europe, constituted a tightly packed racial core such as was not to be met in any other country and such as implied the right to a greater living space [*Lebensraum*] than in the case of other peoples. If, territorially speaking, there existed no political result corresponding to this racial core, that was a consequence of centuries of historical development, and in the continuance of these political conditions lay the greatest danger to the preservation of the German race at its present peak . . . Germany's future was therefore wholly conditional upon the solving of the need for space, and such a solution could be sought, of course, only for a foreseeable period of about one to three generations . . .

Germany's problem could only be solved by means of force and this was never without attendant risk. The campaigns of Frederick the Great for Silesia and Bismarck's wars against Austria and France had involved unheard-of-risk . . . If one accepts as the basis of the following exposition the resort to force with its attendant risks, then there remain still to be answered the questions 'when' and 'how' . . .

Case I: Period 1943–45
After this date only a change for the worse, from our point of view, could be expected.

The equipment of the army, navy and Luftwaffe, as well as the formation of the officer corps, would be nearly completed. Equipment and armament were modern; in further delay there lay the danger of their obsolescence. In particular, the secrecy of 'special weapons' could not be preserved forever. The recruiting of reserves was limited to current age groups; further drafts from older untrained age groups were no longer available . . .

Nobody knew today what the situation would be in the years 1943–45. One thing only was certain, that we could not wait longer.

On the one hand there was the great *Wehrmacht* [armed forces], and the necessity of maintaining it at its present level, the ageing of the movement and of its leaders; and on the other, the prospect of a lowering of the standard of living and of a limitation of the birth rate, which left no choice but to act. If the Führer was still living, it was his unalterable resolve to solve Germany's problem of space at the latest by 1943–45.

Source: Minutes of the conference in the Reich Chancellery, Berlin, 5 November 1937 in HMSO (1949–83: Ser. D, vol. 1, 29–39).

Document 7   PREPARATION FOR WAR BEFORE MUNICH

Most Secret
It is impossible to define in any detail, in advance of the event, the course of action that will have to be adopted by the air striking force at the out-set of a war with Germany. It must depend to a very great extent on the action that

is taken by the German air forces, partly because they have the initiative owing to their superior strength, and partly owing to the policy of His Majesty's Government that we should not initiate air action which may cause heavy loss of life to the civil population.

We must conserve our resources, owing to our shortage of reserves, and that for this and a variety of other reasons we cannot hope for quick or impressive results in the initial stages . . . Taking the above factors into account it is considered that it would be unwise to begin retaliation on the Ruhr until we are in a position to do so effectively. Sporadic and inaccurate bombing of the Ruhr by a few squadrons would be ineffective and generally undesirable. When we attack we must do so effectively, and it is essential that we should be able to destroy the generating stations and coking plants which have been selected as the first and most vital objectives.

It is during this early period when our offensive action is invariably limited, that effective use might be made of dropping propaganda from the air . . . To begin with, therefore, attacks on Germany direct from the United Kingdom must be directed against objectives on the coast and in the extreme North of Germany, with the objects:

(a) of the destruction and dislocation of really important objectives, which will seriously affect the German capacity to carry on the war, and
(b) of forcing the enemy to disperse his active fighter defences between the North of Germany, the French Front and the Czechoslovak Front.

Source: From a memorandum prepared by the British Air Staff, 27 September 1938, PRO AIR 14/225.

THE MUNICH CONFERENCE   **Document 8**

It began by a brief statement by Herr Hitler thanking those present for their acceptances of his invitation and pointing out the need for speedy decisions. Mr Chamberlain replied suitably, as did M. Daladier and Signor Mussolini. Towards the close of his remarks Signor Mussolini said that he thought the best way of making progress was for someone to produce a basis for discussion, and he therefore read the Memorandum. It was evident that this document was a reasonable re-statement of much that had been discussed in the Anglo-French and the Anglo-German conversations, and the Prime Minister was ready to accept it as a basis of discussion by the Conference.

It was, however, the turn of M. Daladier to speak first, and to our relief he at once said he was prepared to adopt Signor Mussolini's document as a basis for discussion. This was agreed . . .

In the course of this discussion the Prime Minister raised the question of the representation at the Conference of the Czech Government. The conclusion was reached that the heads of the four Powers must accept responsibility for deciding – in the circumstances – how the situation should be dealt with . . . The German proposals for evacuation and occupation surprised us by their moderation and by the degree of latitude which they left to the International Commission. They were explained in detail by Herr Hitler by reference to a map, copies of which we were given.

After a short adjournment for dinner, agreement was reached upon the evacuation areas and upon the time-table.

We inserted in the preamble words to show that the Conference had been working in the light of the fact that it had already been agreed in principle that the Sudeten German areas should be ceded . . .

After very long delays due to inefficient organisation and lack of control, the Agreement and supplementaries were signed a little before 2 a.m. on the 30th September, and the proceedings concluded by brief expressions of satisfaction.

Source: Note by Sir H. Wilson on the Munich Conference, 29–30 September 1938, in HMSO (1946–82: 3rd Ser., vol. 2, 631–3).

Document 9   THE MUNICH AGREEMENT

Germany, the United Kingdom, France and Italy, taking into consideration the agreement which has been already reached in principle for the cession to Germany of the Sudeten German territory, have agreed the following terms and conditions thereon, and by this Agreement they hold each themselves responsible for the steps necessary to secure its fulfilment:

1. The evacuation [of Czech forces and officials] will begin on 1st October.

2. The United Kingdom, France and Italy agree that the evacuation of the territory shall be completed by 10th October without any existing installations having been destroyed, and that the Czechoslovak Government will be held responsible for carrying out the evacuation without damage to the said installations.

3. The conditions governing the evacuation will be laid down in detail by an international commission composed of representatives of Germany, the United Kingdom, France, Italy and Czechoslovakia . . .

6. The final determination of the frontier will be carried out by the international commission. This commission will also be entitled to recommend to

the four Powers – Germany, the United Kingdom, France and Italy – in certain exceptional cases minor modifications in the strictly ethnographical determination of the zones which are to be transferred without plebiscite.

7. There will be a right of option into and out of the transferred territories, the option to be exercised within six months from the date of this Agreement. A German-Czechoslovak commission shall determine the details of the option, consider ways of facilitating the transfer of population and settle questions of principle arising out of the said transfer.

8. The Czech Government will, within a period of four weeks from the date of the Agreement, release from their military and police forces any Sudeten Germans who may wish to be released, and the Czech Government will, within the same period, release Sudeten German prisoners who are serving terms of imprisonment for political offences.

Munich, September 29, 1938

Source: Extract from the Munich Agreement between Germany, Britain, Italy and France, Munich 29 September 1938 in Grenville (1974: 187–8).

ECONOMIC PRESSURE ON JAPAN   **Document 10**

For about a hundred years up to the turn of the present century, when the principle of free trade was at its peak . . . if any nation adopted a protectionist policy in contradiction to the free trade policy of the Anglo-American powers, it was ostracized and considered a heretic by advanced countries. For many decades the less-advanced nations were not permitted to close their doors to the economic influences of Great Britain and the United States, and as a result, their industries were prevented from growing and attaining further development, being held back by advanced countries under political as well as economic pressure despite their will to progress.

When the doctrines of freedom of communications and trade prevailed the world over, enabling men and goods to move from one country to another with comparative ease, regardless of the status of their countries, it was possible even for small nations . . . to maintain a respectable existence side by side with great Powers . . . Now, however, that such doctrines have all but disappeared with the great Powers' closing or threatening to close their doors to others, small countries have no other choice left but to strive as best they can to form their own economic *blocs* or to found powerful states, lest their very existence be jeopardized. There can be no just criticism condemning this choice of the small countries . . .

Because of the existence of the idea of economic pressure, which does not seem likely to disappear, the countries which are not economically self-dependent will quite naturally try to find ways and means of defending themselves in anticipation of some crisis and in order to escape coercion in the form of economic pressure. They will consider the formation of economic *blocs* as a measure of economic self-defence, or the establishment of powerful states which can be self-sufficient both in times of peace and war . . . There is no reason why economic self-defence, which is the same [as military self-defence] in its ultimate effects, should not be acknowledged as proper in international relations.

Source: *Contemporary Japan*, vol. 10, January 1941, speech by ex-Foreign Minister Arita, reprinted in Lebra (1975: 74–5).

Document 11 MUSSOLINI'S VISION OF EMPIRE

Never at any time – and especially today, on account of the paralysis of the so-called Conference on unattainable Disarmament [the Disarmament Conference which met at Geneva from 2 February 1932 to 20 November 1934] – was there such a categorical and imperative duty for a nation that must remain alive to keep strong – and even more so in the case of Italy, which must calmly develop the internal, renovating work of the Revolution. It is necessary to be militarily strong, not for aggressive purpose but in order to be able to cope with an emergency . . .

The military power of a state and the future and safety of a nation are linked to the demographical problem, and this poses a serious problem for all countries of the white race, including our own. I must reaffirm once again, and in the most peremptory manner . . . that numbers are the indispensable prerequisite for leadership. Without numerical superiority everything declines, crumbles away, and dies . . . The notion that an increase in population brings about a condition of poverty is so idiotic that it does not even deserve the honour of rebuttal . . .

The historical objectives of Italy have two names: Asia and Africa. South and east are the cardinal points that should excite the interest and determination of Italians. There is little or nothing to do towards the north, and the same is true towards the west, whether it be Europe or overseas. These two objectives of ours are justified by geography and history. Of all the large Western powers of Europe, Italy is the nearest to Africa and to Asia. A few hours by sea and much less by air are enough to link up Italy with Africa and with Asia. Let nobody misunderstand the meaning of this century-old task that I assign to the present and to the future Italian generations. It is not a question of territorial conquests but a natural expansion that should lead to collaboration between Italy and the people of Africa, between Italy and the near East and the Middle East . . .

The aim we have in mind is the development and exploitation of the still-countless resources of these two continents – and especially Africa – and of bringing these areas more closely into the orbit of world civilization. Italy is in a position to accomplish this task. Her location in the Mediterranean, which is resuming its historic role of uniting the East to the West, confers this right and binds Italy to this obligation. We do not intend to claim either monopolies or privileges, but we do claim and we intend to make clear that those countries who arrived ahead of us, those who are satisfied and those who are conservative, should not try to block on every side the spiritual, political and economic expansion of Fascist Italy . . .

But there is one danger that can threaten the Regime, and this may be represented by what is commonly called the 'bourgeois spirit' – that is to say, a spirit of satisfaction and adjustment, a tendency towards scepticism, compromise, an easy life and advancement . . . I do not exclude the existence of the bourgeois temperament, but I deny that those who have it can be Fascists. The creed of the Fascist is heroism, that of the bourgeois is egoism. There is only one remedy against the danger, the principle of continual revolution . . .

The fourth great historical epoch of the Italian people – which future historians will label the Epoch of the Blackshirts – has already begun.

Source: From a speech by Benito Mussolini, 18 March 1934 in Rome in Delzell (1971: 188–90).

HITLER'S DREAM OF WORLD POWER   **Document 12**

'We need space', he almost shrieked, 'to make us independent of every possible political grouping and alliance. In the east, we must have mastery as far as the Caucasus and Iran. In the west, we need the French coast. We need Flanders and Holland. Above all we need Sweden. We must become a colonial power. We must have a sea power equal to that of Britain . . . We cannot, like Bismarck, limit ourselves to national aims. We must rule Europe or fall apart as a nation, fall back into the chaos of small states. Now do you understand why I cannot be limited, either in the east or in the west? . . .

'In the centre I shall place the steely core of a Greater Germany welded into an indissoluble unity. Then Austria, Bohemia and Moravia, western

Poland. A block of one hundred million, indestructible, without a flaw, without an alien element, the firm foundation of our power. Then an eastern alliance: Poland, the Baltic States, the Ukraine, the Volga Basin, Georgia . . . We cannot in any way evade the final battle between German race ideals and pan-Slav mass ideals. Here yawns the eternal abyss which no mutual political interest can bridge. We must win the victory of German race-consciousness over the masses eternally fated to serve and obey. We alone can conquer the great continental space . . . We shall take this struggle upon us. It will open to us the door of permanent mastery of the world.'

Source: Hitler in conversation with Hermann Rauschning, 1934, in Rauschning (1939: 126–37).

Document 13   ECONOMIC APPEASEMENT

But there are many who say that economic appeasement provides the key to our difficulties, and it is certain that with most of our political problems there is an economic problem inextricably intertwined . . . what is a serious danger is the extent to which Germany is moving away from the economic system of Western Europe into an idiosyncrasy of attitude not unlike that of Soviet Russia. To those countries who can supply her needs and will take her goods, such as the countries of the Danubian area, the Balkan States and Turkey, she acts as a strong attraction; and this is not without political danger. If this attraction were developed in the direction of Russia, who can supply so many German needs, the danger might become greater, and a division might establish itself between two economic systems in Western and Eastern Europe. It is, therefore, of urgent importance to restore Germany to her normal place in the Western European system.

Source: Imperial Conference 1937, Memorandum by the Foreign Secretary, in Mommsen and Kettenacker (1983: 164).

Document 14   BRITAIN AND GERMANY IN THE BALKANS

The Prime Minister
What, taking an economic view, is the position of Germany in relation to the States of Central and South-Eastern Europe? Geographically, she must occupy a dominating position there. She does now. As a matter of fact, in so far as those states are agricultural in character, the nature of the trade

between them and Germany is complementary. They can supply Germany with raw materials and foodstuffs in return for articles of manufacture which Germany is so well fitted to supply, but I do not see any reason why we should expect that a fundamental change is likely to take place in those regions . . . So far as this country is concerned, we have no wish to block Germany out from those countries or to encircle her economically . . . Do not let us suppose that there necessarily must be economic warfare between Germany and ourselves . . . I finish what I have to say on this subject by the general observation that, in my view, there is room both for Germany and for us in trade with those countries and that neither of us ought to try to obtain exclusive possession of their markets.

Source: House of Commons Debate, 1 November 1938, in Chamberlain (1939: 338–9).

THE FOUR-YEAR PLAN **Document 15**

I hold it necessary that 100% self-sufficiency be introduced with iron decisiveness in all the areas where this is possible, and through this not only to make the national supply of these most important materials independent of abroad, but that through this can be saved that foreign exchange which we need in peacetime for importing foodstuffs. I would like to emphasise that I see in this task pure economic mobilisation, with no cutting back in armaments firms in peacetime for saving or stockpiling raw materials for war . . . Almost four valuable years have gone by. There is no doubt that we could be independent from abroad already today in the areas of fuel, rubber and partly, too, in iron ore supply. Just as we produce at the moment 7 or 800,000 tons of oil, so we can produce 3 million tons. Just as we manufacture today a few thousand tons of rubber, we could produce 70 or 80,000 tons annually. In the same way as we have increased from $2^{1}/_{2}$ million tons of iron ore output to 7 million, we could process 20 or 25 million tons of German iron ore, and if necessary 30. There has been enough time to ascertain what we cannot do. It is now necessary to work out what we can do.

I therefore lay down the following task:

I The German army must be ready for combat in 4 years.

II The German economy must be capable of war in 4 years.

Source: Hitler's Memorandum on the tasks of the Four-Year Plan, August 1936, in Treue (1955: 209–10) (translated by the author).

Document 16   ECONOMIC DANGERS FOR BRITAIN

We must face hard facts. We cannot finance ourselves by inflationary methods which, if they gave relief for a certain period to an embarrassed Exchequer, would be followed with certainty by a collapse in the purchasing power of our currency, so that the loans we could raise would represent little in buying power. We cannot continue to lose gold in great quantities indefinitely or we shall find ourselves in a position when we should be unable to wage any other war than a brief one. There is a limit to the rate at which we can raise money, and that limit to the best of my judgement, is already reached. We can go on for another six or nine months if there are no further additions, but thereafter, unless something unexpectedly favourable happens, it may well be that the present rate could not be maintained.

Source: The Chancellor of the Exchequer, Sir John Simon, in cabinet, 18 May 1939, in Shay (1977: 276–7).

————————◄●►————————

Document 17   THE CRISIS IN FRANCE

The real trouble started on November 23 1938, first in the north of France, and on the afternoon of the 24th, in the Paris region. That day, while Mr Chamberlain and Lord Halifax – who had already been welcomed at the Gare du Nord on the previous night with loud cries of *A bas Munich* and *Vive Eden!* – were being feted at the Paris Town Hall, a vast stay-in strike broke out at the Renault works with its 33,000 workers. Simultaneously, a number of other works were occupied. The stay-in strike at Renault's was a challenge to the Government; for no Government had ever even attempted to evacuate by armed force a factory even half that size. A year earlier M. Chautemps had sent the *garde mobile* to Colombes to evacuate the much smaller Goodrich Tyre works; but the strikers had threatened to resist; there was danger of serious blood-shed, and the Government withdrew the troops. The strike was ultimately settled after lengthy negotiations. But now there were no longer any Socialists in the Government; and M. Daladier, without even attempting to negotiate an evacuation, sent 10,000 *gardes mobiles* to the Renault works and ordered them to 'chuck the strikers out'. He told them, if necessary, to use tear gas. By midnight the works were cleared, with comparatively little bloodshed.

Source: Werth (1939: 370).

————————◄●►————————

'PEACE FOR OUR TIME'   **Document 18**

a) Anglo-German Declaration, 30 September 1938

We, the German Führer and Chancellor and the British Prime Minister, have had a further meeting today and are agreed in recognizing that the question of Anglo-German relations is of the first importance for the two countries and for Europe.

We regard the agreement signed last night, the Munich Agreement and the Anglo-German Naval Agreement as symbolic of the desire of our two peoples never to go to war with one another again.

We are resolved that the method of consultation shall be the method adopted to deal with any other questions that may concern our two countries, and we are determined to continue our efforts to remove possible sources of difference and thus to contribute to assure the peace of Europe.

Source: Chamberlain (1939: 189).

b) Franco-German Declaration, 6 December 1938

1. The German Government and the French Government fully share the conviction that peaceful and good neighbourly relations between Germany and France constitute one of the most essential elements in the consolidation of the situation in Europe and in the preservation of general peace. Both Governments will consequently do all within their power to assure the development in this direction of the relations between their countries.

Source: HMSO (1949–83: Ser. D, vol. 4, 470).

THE CHANGE OF MOOD IN THE WEST   **Document 19**

A year ago we had undertaken no specific commitments on the Continent of Europe beyond those which had then existed for some considerable time and are familiar to you all. Today we are bound by new agreements for mutual defence with Poland and Turkey: we have guaranteed assistance to Greece and Roumania against aggression, and we are now engaged with the Soviet Government in a negotiation, to which I hope there may very shortly be a successful issue, with a view to associating them with us for the defence of the States of Europe whose independence and neutrality may be threatened. We have assumed obligations, and are preparing to assume more, with full understanding of their consequences. We know that, if the security and independence of other countries are to disappear, our own security and our own independence will be gravely threatened. We know that, if international law and order is to be preserved, we must be prepared to fight in its defence.

In the past we have always stood out against the attempt by any single Power to dominate Europe at the expense of the liberties of other nations, and British policy is, therefore, only following the inevitable line of its own history, if such an attempt were to be made again . . . The threat of military force is holding the world to ransom, and our immediate task is to resist aggression. I would emphasise that tonight with all the strength at my command, so that nobody may misunderstand it.

Source: Speech by Lord Halifax at Chatham House, 29 June 1939, in HMSO (1939: 58–65).

Document 20   HITLER PLANS TO CRUSH POLAND

Our situation *vis-à-vis* the surrounding world has remained the same. Germany was outside the circle of the Great Powers. A balance of power has been established without Germany's participation.

This balance is being disturbed by Germany claiming her vital rights and her reappearance in the circle of the Great Powers. All claims are regarded as 'breaking in' . . .

Living space proportionate to the greatness of the State is fundamental to every Power. One can do without it for a time but sooner or later the problems will have to be solved by hook or by crook. The alternatives are rise or decline. In fifteen or twenty years' time the solution will be forced upon us. No German statesman can shirk the problem for longer . . .

The Pole is not a fresh enemy. Poland will always be on the side of our adversaries. In spite of treaties of friendship Poland has always been bent on exploiting every opportunity against us.

It is not Danzig that is at stake. For us it is a matter of expanding our living space in the east and making food supplies secure and also solving the problem of the Baltic States. Food supplies can only be obtained from thinly populated areas. Over and above fertility, the thorough German cultivation will tremendously increase the produce.

No other openings can be seen in Europe . . . There is therefore no question of sparing Poland and we are left with the decision:

To attack Poland at the first suitable opportunity.

We cannot expect a repetition of Czechoslovakia. There will be war. Our task is to isolate Poland. Success in isolating her will be decisive.

Therefore the Führer must reserve to himself the final order to strike. It must not come to a simultaneous showdown with the West (France and England).

Source: Report on the Führer's conference with the heads of the armed forces, 23 May 1939, in HMSO (1949–83: Ser. D, vol. 6, 575–6).

CHAMBERLAIN GUARANTEES POLAND **Document 21**

I am glad to take this opportunity of stating again the general policy of His Majesty's Government. They have constantly advocated the adjustment, by way of free negotiation between the parties concerned, of any differences that may arise between them. They consider that this is the natural and proper course where differences exist. In their opinion there should be no question incapable of solution by peaceful means and they would see no justification for the substitution of force or threats of force for the method of negotiation.

. . . I now have to inform the House that in the event of any action which clearly threatened Polish independence, and which the Polish government accordingly considered it vital to resist with their national forces, His Majesty's Government would feel themselves bound at once to lend the Polish Government all support in their power. They have given the Polish Government an assurance to this effect.

Source: HMSO (1946–82: 3rd Ser., vol. 4, 553).

THE FRANCO-BRITISH 'WAR PLAN', 1939 **Document 22**

The USA would be a friendly neutral . . . not likely to intervene actively unless at a later stage.

The Soviet Union would probably be unwilling to intervene actively except in the event of a direct threat to herself, but she may be expected to exercise a restraining influence on Japan. Japan would be unlikely at first to join our enemies openly, but would be sure to intensify her campaign against British interests in the Far East, and likely to enter the war if the allies were in serious danger of defeat . . .

Spain must remain neutral.

It would be unwise to place any substantial reliance on assistance, active or passive, from Poland.

The lesser European powers, though predominantly sympathetic toward the Allies, would probably attempt to remain neutral . . . The Allies would have greater financial resources than Germany. They are superior at sea . . .

Once we had been able to develop the full fighting strength of the British and French Empires, we should regard the outcome of the war with confidence.

Source: British Strategical Memorandum for Anglo-French Staff Conversations, 20 March 1939, prepared for the Chiefs-of-Staff, PRO AIR 9/105, 6–7, 41.

Document 23   BRITISH INTELLIGENCE ON GERMANY

Let us examine firstly Germany's situation at the moment. From the point of view of the German Army it is extremely unsound. A considerable proportion of the active Army – unmobilised and in many cases under peace strength – is scattered throughout Moravia and Bohemia, with elements in Slovakia. It must be at least several months before the Germans can hope to produce units or formations with the help of arms they have acquired from the Czechs. The process will call for the services of many officers and NCOs who can ill be spared from the active German army . . . If we can only convince our potential allies in the east of the patent fact that Germany is in no position to fight a major war now with any hope of evading inevitable and swift strangulation, there seems every reason why we should do our best to produce a situation leading to such a war and definitely welcome it. It is indeed, in my opinion, the only sound solution to the problem with which we are faced . . . Nothing but the internal disruption of Germany can save us. Have we any right to consider such disruption more than an outside possibility?

It is true that grave elements of discontent within the country exist. But to produce the organised resistance to the Party or dissension within its ranks which can alone produce disruption, something more than a continuation or even an appreciable increase in the present perfectly bearable 'hardships' and inconveniences under which the German people suffer is required. War, and war now with a 'near' eastern front, would hit them hard and quickly and might well produce the hoped-for results. Without war, and with increasing benefits from Germany's eastern neighbours, these results may never be achieved.

Source: Memorandum on the German military situation by the Military Attaché in Berlin, 28 March 1939, in HMSO (1946–82: 3rd Ser., vol. 4, 623–7).

STALIN WARNS THE WEST AFTER MUNICH   **Document 24**

Similarly, in matters of foreign policy, account is taken of the realities of the situation and, above all, of the fact that, in the present state of the Red army, of the Soviet economic system and of Soviet transport, the Soviet Union should avoid intervention in a conflict of capitalistic powers. Thus, while M. Stalin and various other speakers at the Congress emphasise Soviet readiness to defend the frontiers of the Soviet Union, should they be attacked, the line taken by all of them is that the chief care of those responsible for Soviet foreign policy must be to prevent the Soviet Union from being dragged into the struggle now in progress between the Fascist states and the so-called democracies. M. Stalin did, of course, say that the Soviet Union would be prepared to support all peoples who had been the victims of aggression and who were fighting for their national independence. This, however, may merely imply that the Soviet Government would be prepared, as in the case of China and Republican Spain, to provide assistance in the form of war material, provisions and technical help, after aggression was in full swing. Those innocents at home who believe that Soviet Russia is only awaiting an invitation to join the Western democracies should be advised to ponder M. Stalin's advice to his party:

'To be cautious and not allow Soviet Russia to be drawn into conflicts by warmongers who are accustomed to have others pull the chestnuts out of the fire.'

Source: Report from the British ambassador in Moscow to the foreign secretary, 20 March 1939, in HMSO (1946–82: 3rd Ser., vol. 4, 419).

THE FRANCO-BRITISH FAILURE IN MOSCOW   **Document 25**

We have now conferred for five successive days and have discussed a great variety of subjects but have not yet found a single point on which we can reach a definite agreement. The initial conditions under which we started were not favourable to success. The French Ambassador, who is shrewd and intelligent, expressed the opinion when we arrived that the duration of our stay would be either two days or two years. Soviet Russians speak contemptuously of Britain and France as the yielding (or surrendering) Powers. We have up to the present been very polite and have made one or two concessions to them on points of procedure. I think they hold the opinion that Britain and France are in a hurry to reach an agreement and that suitable pressure will obtain the necessary concessions. The way they hand us their demands (not requests) is somewhat in the manner of a victorious Power dictating terms to a beaten enemy.

2. They make it plain that in their opinion we come here as suppliants asking them to give us a Treaty of assistance. In consequence, any unpleasant jobs to be done must be done by us. They demand that if the Soviet armies are to help the Allies, Britain and France must obtain the approval of Poland and Roumania for Soviet armies to move through their territory in the desired directions . . .

5. It is difficult to say how much their behaviour is based on tactics or bluff. It is evident that they attach immense importance to getting a favourable reply from Poland and Roumania. They have once or twice threatened that the continuation of our discussions would be useless if an early reply is not received. *Pro tem*, they still continue to discuss, but they seem to have no desire to conclude an early agreement unless on terms entirely in accordance with their demands . . .

7. Judged from our experience to date, it would seem that unless there is a sudden change, agreement on the many points discussed may take months to achieve.

August 17th 1939.

14. Today Voroshilov [Soviet Commissar for Defence] remarked that he looked on a European war as a certainty; he also considered that the situation today is definitely worse than when we first met on Saturday, August 12th. Since he seems clearly to be in no hurry to conclude a military or any other agreement unless on the basis of his cardinal point, it would appear that he is fairly well content with the other alternative, viz. sit on the fence and remain neutral while the remainder of us cut one another's throats.

Source: Letter from Admiral Reginald Plunkett-Ernle-Erle-Drax [head of the British delegation in Moscow] to Admiral Lord Chatfield, 16 August 1939 in HMSO (1946–82: 3rd Ser., vol. 7, 32–5).

Document 26   THE SOVIET REACTION TO GERMAN ADVANCES, 1939

a) Germany is prepared to discuss and come to an understanding with us on all questions that both sides are interested in, and to give all the security guarantees which we would require from them. Even in relation to the Baltic countries and Poland it would be easy to come to an agreement, as it would in relation to the Ukraine (which Germany would leave alone). To my question about how confident he was that his words reflected the mood and intention of higher circles, Schnurre [Dr Karl Schnurre, German trade negotiator] said that he spoke on the direct instructions of Ribbentrop . . .

Germany was prepared to give us a choice of everything from friendship to enmity. Naturally, we didn't give Schnurre any hopes, limiting ourselves to general noises and promising to bring the talks to your attention.

Source: Georgi Astakhov, Soviet Chargé d'Affaires, to Soviet Foreign Affairs Commissariat, 27 July 1939.

b) [The Germans] are obviously worried by our negotiations with the British and French military and they have become unsparing in their arguments and promises in order to prevent a military agreement. For the sake of this they are now ready, I believe, to make the kind of declarations and gestures that would have been inconceivable six months ago. The Baltic, Bessarabia, Eastern Poland (not to speak of the Ukraine) – at the present time this is the minimum they would give up without a long discussion in order to secure a promise from us not to intervene in their conflict with Poland.

Source: Astakhov to Soviet Foreign Commissariat, 12 August 1939. Both extracts from Roberts (1995: 80, 88).

THE GERMAN-SOVIET PACT   **Document 27**

23rd August 1939

Guided by the desire to strengthen the cause of peace between the USSR and Germany, and proceeding from the fundamental stipulations of the neutrality treaty concluded in April 1926, the Government of the USSR and the Government of Germany have come to the following agreement:

Article 1. The two contracting parties undertake to refrain from any act of force, any aggressive act, or any attack against each other, either individually or in conjunction with other Powers.

Article 2. If one of the contracting parties should become the object of hostilities on the part of a third Power, the other contracting party will give no support of any kind to that third Power.

Secret Additional Protocol

On the occasion of the signature of the non-aggression treaty between the German Reich and the USSR, the undersigned plenipotentiaries of the two parties discussed in strictly confidential conversations the question of the delimitation of their respective spheres of interest in Eastern Europe. These conversations led to the following result:

1. In the event of a territorial and political transformation in the territories belonging to the Baltic states, the northern frontier of Lithuania shall

represent the frontier of the spheres of interest both of Germany and the USSR . . .

2. In the event of a territorial and political transformation of the territories belonging to the Polish State, the spheres of interest of both Germany and the USSR shall be bounded approximately by the line of the rivers Narev, Vistula and San . . .

3. With regard to South-Eastern Europe, the Soviet side emphasizes its interest in Bessarabia.

Source: Treaty of Non-Aggression between the USSR and Germany, in Degras (1951–3: vol. 3, 359–61).

Document 28   HITLER GAMBLES ON WESTERN WEAKNESS

Now it is also a great risk. Iron nerves, iron resolution.

The following special reasons strengthen my idea. England and France are obligated, neither is in a position for it. There is no actual rearmament in England, just propaganda . . . The English speak of a war of nerves. It is one element of this war of nerves to present an increase in armament. But how is British rearmament in actual fact? The construction programme of the Navy for 1938 has not yet been filled. Only mobilization of the reserve fleet. Purchase of fishing steamers. Considerable strengthening of the Navy, not before 1941 or 1942.

Little has been done on land. England will be able to send a maximum of 3 divisions to the continent. A little has been done for the air force, but it is only a beginning . . . England does not want the conflict to break out for two or three years . . . England's position in the world is very precarious. She will not accept any risks.

France lacks men (decline of the birth rate). Little has been done for rearmament. The artillery is antiquated. France did not want to enter on this adventure . . .

The enemy had another hope, that Russia would become our enemy after the conquest of Poland. The enemy did not count on my great power of resolution. Our enemies are little worms. I saw them at Munich.

Source: Führer's speech to the Commanders-in-Chief, 22 August 1939, in International Military Tribunal (1947: vol. 3, 584–5).

THE LAST GASP OF APPEASEMENT   **Document 29**

21st July 1939

The programme discussed by Herr Wohlthat and Sir Horace Wilson was as follows: (a) political points; (b) military points; (c) economic points . . . Herr Wilson suggested as the general objective a broad Anglo-German agreement on all major questions, as had been originally envisaged by the Führer. In this way questions of such great importance would be raised and settled that the deadlocked Near Eastern questions, such as Danzig and Poland, would be pushed into the background and become immaterial. Sir Horace Wilson definitely told Herr Wohlthat that the conclusion of a non-aggression pact would enable Britain to rid herself of her commitments vis-à-vis Poland. As a result the Polish problem would lose much of its acuteness . . .

Sir Horace Wilson further said that it was contemplated holding new elections in Britain this autumn. From the point of view of purely domestic political tactics, it was all one to the Government whether the elections were held under the cry 'Be Ready for a Coming War!' or under the cry 'A Lasting Understanding With Germany in Prospect and Achievable!'. It could obtain the backing of the electors for either of these cries and assure its rule for another five years. Naturally, it preferred the peaceful cry.

Source: Memorandum by the German Ambassador in London, von Dirksen, 21 July 1939, about unofficial conversations on an Anglo-German agreement, in Royal Institute of International Affairs (1929–54: 1939–46, vol. 1, 324–6).

BONNET'S DOUBTS ABOUT WAR   **Document 30**

I learned of the Germano-Soviet [sic] Pact during the morning of the 23rd August and immediately concluded that a revision of the diplomatic situation was the order of the day. Stalin had given Hitler a free hand and hoped to see the nations of Europe embroiled in war while the USSR stayed on the sideline and prepared itself for the role of arbiter . . .

To me Stalin's intentions seemed perfectly clear, and I feared any attempt to save Poland would only lead to that country's complete destruction, and seriously compromise France's permanent interests.

The situation had to be examined afresh. We had to reconsider our engagements to Poland, begin discussions with her and with England . . . The Germano-Soviet Pact broke the power equilibrium to the benefit of our adversaries. It allowed Stalin, in the event of war, to stay outside the conflict, to keep his forces intact, and to impose Communism in Europe and Asia, perhaps throughout the world.

Such an extremity had to be warded off at any price. I explained my ideas to Daladier [French Prime Minister] on the morning of the 23rd after having summarized them for my colleagues at the Quai [the French Foreign Office]. I asked Daladier to call a meeting of the Committee for National Defence so that the leaders of our armed force could give us their advice on the capital question – 'Given that the Russians fail us, what are our chances of winning a war? And, would it be wise to seek a peaceful compromise?'

. . . the Committee gave a negative answer to my first question, 'Is it in France's military interests to reconsider the situation and use the time gained to strengthen our armed force?'

I then put the question: 'Are our army, navy and air force in a condition for us to keep our engagements to Poland?' The reply, and for all three arms, was an unconditional 'Yes' . . . The situation, then, was that on the 23rd of August we still had a chance of extricating ourselves, still had a chance to turn our backs on war – *on the grounds that we had not managed to get Russian co-operation* [italics in original]. In that way we would have turned the tables on Stalin, whose manoeuvring had literally given Hitler a free hand in the West. But Gamelin's [Chief of the French General Staff] advice, and its acceptance by the Defence Committee, ended that hope.

Source: Extract from Bonnet (1965: 252–7).

Document 31   POLAND IN THE MIDDLE

Following 'authoritative' indication was publication this morning of Polish attitude regarding Danzig. Poland would regard as a violation of her rights

(a) any attempt to incorporate Danzig in Reich

(b) exclusion of Danzig from Polish customs territory

(c) control of Polish rights in Danzig by a third Power

(d) deprivation of Polish minority in Danzig of rights of national development . . .

Attitude of Polish Government would depend on changes made. If their aim were contrary to any of these four fundamental points Polish government would draw appropriate conclusions and act accordingly.

Source: Sir H. Kennard in Warsaw to Lord Halifax, 25 August 1939, in HMSO (1946–82: 3rd Ser., vol. 7, 236–7).

THE LAST DAYS OF PEACE   **Document 32**

August 31, 1939. An ugly awakening. Attolico [Italian Ambassador in Berlin] telegraphs at nine, saying that the situation is desperate and that unless something new comes up there will be war in a few hours. I go quickly to the Palazzo Venezia. We must find a new solution. In agreement with the Duce I telephone Halifax to tell him that the Duce can intervene with Hitler only if he brings a fat prize: Danzig. Empty handed he can do nothing . . . As a last resort let us propose to France and Great Britain a conference for September 5th, for the purpose of reviewing those clauses of the Treaty of Versailles which disturb Europe . . . Halifax receives it favourably, reserving the right to submit it to Chamberlain.

Sept 2, 1939. Yielding to French pressure we suggest to Berlin the possibilities of a conference. A mere hint for the information of Berlin. Contrary to what I expected, Hitler does not reject the proposal absolutely. I inform the Duce. I call in the French and British ambassadors. I telephone personally to Lord Halifax and to Bonnet. I find much goodwill among the French, and maybe as much among the British, but with greater firmness. One condition is put forward: the evacuation of the Polish territories occupied by the Germans.

It seems to me that nothing else need be done. It isn't my business to give Hitler advice that he would reject decisively, and maybe with contempt . . . The last note of hope has died. Daladier talks to the French Chamber in a decisive tone, and his English colleagues do the same in London . . .

September 3, 1939 . . . At eleven o'clock the news arrives that Great Britain has declared war on Germany. France does the same at 5 p.m. . . . I am not a military man, I do not know how the war will develop, but I know one thing – it will develop, and it will be long, uncertain and relentless. The participation of Great Britain makes this certain. England has made this declaration to Hitler. The war can end only with Hitler's elimination or the defeat of Britain.

Source: Excerpts from Count Ciano's diary, 31 August to 3 September 1939, in Muggeridge (1947: 140–4).

CHAMBERLAIN'S 'AWFUL SUNDAY'   **Document 33**

September 10 1939

The final long-drawn-out agonies that preceded the actual declaration of war were as nearly unendurable as could be. We were anxious to bring things to a head, but there were three complications – the secret communications that were going on with Goering and Hitler through a neutral intermediary, the conference proposal of Mussolini, and the French anxiety to postpone the actual declaration as long as possible, until they could evacuate their women and children, and mobilise their armies. There was very little of this that we could say in public . . .

The communications with Hitler and Goering looked rather promising at one time, but came to nothing in the end, as Hitler apparently got carried away by the prospect of a short war in Poland, and then a settlement . . . They gave the impression, probably with intention, that it was possible to persuade Hitler to accept a peaceful and reasonable solution of the Polish question, in order to get an Anglo-German agreement, which he continually declared to be his greatest ambition.

What happened to destroy this chance? Was Hitler merely talking through his hat, and deliberately deceiving us while he matured his schemes? I don't think so. There is good evidence that orders for the invasion on the 25th August were actually given and then cancelled at the last moment because H. wavered. With such an extraordinary creature one can only speculate. But I believe he did seriously contemplate an agreement with us, and that he worked seriously at proposals (subsequently broadcast) which to his one-track mind seemed almost fabulously generous. But at the last moment some brainstorm took possession of him – maybe Ribbentrop stirred it up – and once he had set his machine in motion, he couldn't stop it . . . Mussolini's proposals were, I think, a perfectly genuine attempt to stop war, not for any altruistic reasons, but because Italy was not in a state to go to war and exceedingly likely to get into trouble if other people did. But it was doomed to failure, because Hitler by that time was not prepared to hold his hand, unless he could get what he wanted without war. And we weren't prepared to give it to him . . .

So the war began, after a short and troubled night, and only the fact that one's mind works at three times its ordinary pace on such occasions enabled me to get through my broadcast, the formation of the war cabinet, the meeting of the House of Commons, and the preliminary orders on that awful Sunday, which the calendar tells me was this day a week ago . . .

Source: Letter from the Prime Minister, in Feiling (1946: 416–17).

Document 34   BERLIN PROPOSES PEACE

Berlin, October 6

Hitler delivered his much advertised 'peace proposals' in the Reichstag at noon to-day. I went over and watched the show. He delivered his 'peace proposals', and they were almost identical with those I've heard him offer from the same rostrum after every conquest he has made since the march into the Rhineland in 1936 . . . Hitler offered peace in the west if Britain and France stay out of Germany's *Lebensraum* in eastern Europe. The future of Poland he left in doubt, though he said Poland would never again endanger German interests. In other words, a slave Poland, similar to the present slave Bohemia.

Hitler was calmer than usual. There was much joviality but little enthusiasm among the rubber-stamp Reichstag deputies . . . Most of the deputies I talked to afterwards took for granted that peace was assured. It was a lovely fall day, cold and sunny, which seemed to contribute to everybody's good feelings.

Source: William Shirer in his diary, 6 October 1939, in Shirer (1941: 185–6).

THE TRIPARTITE PACT   **Document 35**

The Governments of Germany, Italy and Japan consider it the prerequisite of a lasting peace that every nation in the world shall receive the space to which it is entitled. They have, therefore, decided to stand by and co-operate with one another in their efforts in Greater East Asia and the regions of Europe respectively. In doing this it is their prime purpose to establish and maintain a new order of things . . .

Article 1. Japan recognizes and respects the leadership of Germany and Italy in the establishment of a new order in Europe.

Article 2. Germany and Italy recognize and respect the leadership of Japan in the establishment of a new order in Greater East Asia.

Article 3. Germany, Italy and Japan agree to co-operate in their efforts on aforesaid lines. They further undertake to assist one another with all political, economic, and military means, if one of the three Contracting Powers is attacked by a Power at present not involved in the European War or in the Chinese-Japanese conflict . . .

Article 5. Germany, Italy, and Japan affirm that the above agreement affects in no way the political status existing at present between each of the three Contracting Parties and Soviet Russia.

Source: Three-Power Pact between Germany, Italy, and Japan, signed at Berlin, 27 September 1940, in Jones (1954: 469).

Document 36   PREPARATION FOR TOTAL MOBILIZATION IN GERMANY

The war requires the greatest efforts for building up armament. The High Command of the Armed Forces after consultation with the offices involved has recommended the following guidelines, which have as their object the strongest supply of economic resources in the service of national defence . . . Labour resources and factory capacity, which are not engaged with the production of war goods or essential goods, are to be made available insofar as they can be employed for strengthening armaments.

Source: Goering's decree 'on guidelines for the co-ordination of all resources to increase production for the armed forces', 29 November 1939, Speer Collection, Imperial War Museum, FD 5445/45.

———————◀●▶———————

Document 37   THE BARBAROSSA DIRECTIVE

Directive No 21 'Barbarossa'

The German Armed Forces must be prepared, even before the end of the war against England, to overthrow Soviet Russia in a rapid campaign (Operation 'Barbarossa').

The Army will have to employ for this all available troops, with the limitation that the occupied territories must be secured against surprise.

For the Air Force it will be a case of releasing for the Eastern campaign sufficient strength for the support of the Army, so that a speedy conclusion can be relied on, and so that the damage by hostile air attacks to the Eastern German areas remains as small as possible . . .

The preparation of the High Commands are to be on the following basis: I. General intentions. The main body of the Russian Army stationed in Western Russia must be destroyed in both operations by the driving forward of armoured wedges and the withdrawal of combat units into the depths of Russia must be prevented. By rapid pursuit a line is to be reached from which the Russian Air Force can no longer attack Reich territory. The goal of the operation is a screen against Asiatic Russia from the general line Volga-Archangel. Then the last industrial area remaining to Russia in the Urals can in case of need be knocked out by the Luftwaffe.

Source: Hitler's Directive No. 21 for the invasion of the Soviet Union, 18 December 1940, in Mallmann Showell (1990: 159).

———————◀●▶———————

THE GERMAN ATTACK ON RUSSIA **Document 38**

The Führer gives me a comprehensive explanation of the situation: the attack on Russia will begin as soon as all our troops are in position. This will be sometime in the course of next week. The campaign in Greece cost us dear in matériel, and this is why it is taking somewhat longer than anticipated. They have about 180–200 divisions at their disposal, perhaps rather fewer, in any case about the same as we. And so far as personnel and equipment are concerned, there is no comparison with our forces. The first thrust will be executed at various points. The enemy will be driven back in one, smooth movement. The Führer estimates that the operation will take four months, I reckon on fewer. Bolshevism will collapse like a house of cards. We face victories unequalled in human history.

We must act. Moscow intends to keep out of the war until Europe is exhausted and bled white. Then Stalin will move to bolshevise Europe and impose his own rule. We shall upset his calculations with one stroke . . . We shall fight until Russia's military power no longer exists. Japan is with us. The operation is also necessary from her point of view. Tokyo would never become involved with the USA with Russia intact to her rear. Another reason why Russia must be destroyed. England would like to maintain Russia as a surety for the future of Europe. That was the reason for Cripps' mission to Moscow. It failed. But Russia would attack us if we were weak, and then we would face a two-front war, which we are avoiding by this pre-emptive strike . . . The Führer says: right or wrong, we must win. It is the only way.

Source: Goebbels in his diary, 16 June 1941, in Taylor (1982: 413–15).

RUSSIA RAISES THE PRICE FOR CO-OPERATION **Document 39**

The Soviet Union is prepared to accept the draft of the Four-Power Pact which the Reich Foreign Minister outlined in the conversation of 13th November, regarding political collaboration and reciprocal economic support, subject to the following conditions:

1. Provided that the German troops are immediately withdrawn from Finland, which, under the agreements of 1939, belongs to the Soviet Union's sphere of influence . . .
2. Provided that within the next few months the security of the Soviet Union in the Straits is assured by the conclusion of a mutual assistance pact between the Soviet Union and Bulgaria, which geographically is situated inside the security zone of the Black Sea boundaries of the

Soviet Union, and by the establishment of a base for land and naval forces of the USSR within range of the Bosphorus and the Dardanelles on a long-term lease.

3. Provided that the area south of Batum and Baku in the general direction of the Persian Gulf is recognized as the focal point of the aspirations of the Soviet Union.

Source: Statement by Molotov to the German Ambassador on the proposed Four-Power Pact, 25 November 1940, in Degras (1951–3: vol. 3, 447–8).

Document 40   JAPAN DECIDES ON WAR

Agenda 'Outline of National Policies in View of the Changing Situation'

Policy

1. Our Empire is determined to follow a policy that will result in the establishment of the Greater East Asia Co-prosperity Sphere and will thereby contribute to world peace, no matter what changes may occur in the world situation.

2. Our Empire will continue its efforts to effect a settlement of the China Incident, and will seek to establish a solid basis for the security and preservation of the nation. This will involve 'taking steps to advance south, and, depending on changes in the situation, will involve a settlement of the Northern Question as well.

3. Our Empire is determined to remove all obstacles in order to achieve the above mentioned objectives . . .

In order to achieve the above objectives, preparations for war with Great Britain and the United States will be made . . . In carrying out the plans outlined above, our Empire will not be deterred by the possibility of being involved in a war with Great Britain and the United States.

Source: Imperial Conference, 2 July 1941, in Ike (1967: 78).

Document 41   CREATING THE NEW WORLD ORDER

After a brief outline of the situation on the Eastern front, the Reich Foreign Minister came on to speak about the situation in East Asia.

Ambassador Oshima observed in this regard that Japan's preparations for military action concerned both the south in the direction of Singapore and the north against the Soviet Union, though of course the difficulty arose that both actions could not be undertaken at the same time.

The Reich Foreign Minister expressed the view that it was not necessary for Japan to carry out actions in the north and south simultaneously . . . The worry openly dominating certain circles in Japan that America could become involved in a Japanese-Soviet-Russian conflict, the Reich Foreign Minister considered to be unfounded. America would certainly not come in in such a confrontation. The situation in Soviet Russia is such that even now Stalin is having to fight with the greatest difficulties and his position would certainly in the end reach breaking point if Japan also seized eastern Siberia. It would be best, for this reason, if Japan decided now, this autumn, on such a course of action, for only thus could it free its back in order to turn later with all its strength against the south and capture the Netherlands-Indies and Singapore.

Fear about America, continued the Reich Foreign Minister, is altogether unfounded. The whole American policy represents a great bluff . . . In domestic politics Roosevelt lacks the preconditions for entry into the war for the majority of the American public want to have nothing to do with it . . .

The situation facing Japan now is that Germany will destroy first Russia and then later England. That will happen under any circumstances, independent of the question of Japanese involvement. But Japan could naturally lighten the task of reaching these objectives if it used the opportunity to attack Russia this year. In the following spring it could then turn against the Netherlands-Indies. Otherwise Japan is left with no other choice than either to give up all claims, which in the global situation amounts to self-destruction, or to get stuck in. However the desirable thing is that Germany and Japan shake hands somewhere along the Trans-siberian railway, for even if the war with Russia does not lead this year to the complete collapse of Soviet Russia, the Führer under all circumstances will carry on until this collapse occurs. If the Russian threat finally falls away, the Japanese in east Asia and we in Europe could carry through the New Order without hindrance . . . A thousand-year friendship between Germany and Japan could be constructed on it. The future then yields only one task, to hold America in check, so that it was unable to disturb the New Order.

Source: Minutes of a conversation between the Reich Foreign Minister, von Ribbentrop, and the Japanese Ambassador, General Oshima, on 23 August 1941 in *Akten zur Deutschen auswärtigen Politik*, Ser. D, vol. 8 Part II: 839–40 (translated by the author).

References

Primary sources

Chamberlain, N., *The Struggle for Peace*, Hutchinson, 1939.

Degras, J. (ed.), *Soviet Documents on Foreign Policy*, 3 vols, Oxford University Press, 1951–3.

HMSO, *Documents concerning German-Polish Relations and the Outbreak of Hostilities between Britain and Germany*, HMSO, 1939.

HMSO, *Documents on British Foreign Policy*, 2nd Ser., vols 1–19, 3rd Ser., vols 1–9, HMSO, 1946–82.

HMSO, *Documents on German Foreign Policy*, Ser. C, vols 1–6, Ser. D, vols 1–13, HMSO, 1949–83.

Grenville, J. (ed.), *The Major International Treaties 1914–1973*, Methuen, 1974.

Ike, N. (ed.), *Japan's Decision for War. Records of the 1941 Policy Conferences*, Stanford University Press, 1967.

International Military Tribunal, Nuremberg Trials, *Nazi Conspiracy and Aggression*, 8 vols, State Department, Washington D.C., 1947.

Lebra, J.C., *Japan's Greater East Asia Co-Prosperity Sphere in World War II: selected readings and documents*, Oxford University Press, 1975.

Mallmann Showell, J., *Fuehrer Conferences on Naval Affairs, 1939–1945*, Greenhill Books, 1990.

Ministry of Foreign Affairs, *Documents diplomatiques français*, Ser. 1, vols 1–11, Ser. 2, vols 1–15, Ministry of Foreign Affairs, Paris, 1963–81.

Ministry of Foreign Affairs, *The French Yellow Book*, Hutchinson, 1940.

Roosevelt, F., *The Public Papers and Addresses of Franklin D. Roosevelt*, 13 vols, Macmillan, 1938–50.

Royal Institute of International Affairs, *Documents on International Affairs*, Oxford University Press, 1929–54.

Treue, W. (ed.), 'Denkschrift Hitlers über die Aufgaben eines Vierjahresplans', *Vierteljahrshefte für Zeitgeschichte*, Institut für Zeitgeschichte, Munich, 1955.

US Department of State, *Foreign Relations of the United States*, Department of State, Washington, 1933–41.

Memoirs, diaries and contemporary accounts

Beck, J., *Dernier rapport; politique polonaise 1926–39*, Editions de la Baconnière, Neuchâtel, 1951.

Bonnet, G., *De Munich à la guerre; défense de la paix*, Plon, Paris, 1967.

Bonnet, G., *Quai D'Orsay: 45 Years of French Foreign Policy*, Times Press, Isle of Man, 1965.

Dahlerus, B., *The Last Attempt*, Hutchinson, 1948.

Dilks, D. (ed.), *The Diaries of Sir Alexander Cadogan*, Cassell, 1971.

Dirksen, H. von, *Moscow, Tokyo, London: Twenty Years of German Foreign Policy*, Hutchinson, 1951.

Gladwyn, Lord, *The Memoirs of Lord Gladwyn*, Weidenfeld and Nicolson, 1972.

Grew, J.C., *Ten Years in Japan*, Hammond, 1944.

Halifax, Lord, *Fulness of Days*, Collins, 1957.

Harvey, O., *The Diplomatic Diaries of Oliver Harvey 1937–1940*, ed. Harvey, J., Collins, 1970.

Henderson, N., *Failure of a Mission*, Hodder and Stoughton, 1940.

Hitler, A., *Hitler's Secret Book*, ed. Taylor, T., Grove Press, New York, 1961.

Hitler, A., *Mein Kampf*, ed. Watt, D.C., Hutchinson, 1969.

Hull, C., *Memoirs*, 2 vols, Hodder and Stoughton, 1948.

Leith-Ross, F., *Money Talks: Fifty Years of International Finance*, Hutchinson, 1968.

Lipski, J., *Diplomat in Berlin 1933–1939*, Columbia University Press, 1968.

Lukasiewicz, J., *Diplomat in Paris 1936–1939*, Columbia University Press, 1970.

Maisky, I., *Before the Storm: Recollections*, Hutchinson, 1944.

Muggeridge, M. (ed.), *Ciano's Diary 1938–1943*, Heinemann, 1947.

Rauschning, H., *Hitler Speaks*, Butterworth, 1939.

Reynaud, P., *In the Thick of the Fight 1930–1945*, Cassell, 1955.

Ribbentrop, J. von, *The Ribbentrop Memoirs*, Weidenfeld and Nicolson, 1954.

Schacht, H., *Account Settled*, Weidenfeld and Nicolson, 1949.

Shirer, W., *Berlin Diary 1934–1941*, Hamish Hamilton, 1941.

Taylor, F. (ed.), *The Goebbels Diaries 1939–1941*, Hamish Hamilton, 1982.

Templewood, Viscount, *Nine Troubled Years*, Collins, 1954.

Secondary sources: books

Adamthwaite, A., *France and the Coming of the Second World War*, Frank Cass, 1977.

Adamthwaite, A., *Grandeur and Misery: France's Bid for Power in Europe 1914–1940*, Arnold, 1995.

Aldrich, R., *Greater France: A History of French Overseas Expansion*, Macmillan, 1996.

Andrew, C. and Kanya-Forstner, A., *France Overseas. The Great War and the Climax of French Imperial Expansion*, Thames and Hudson, 1981.

Aster, S., *1939: the Making of the Second World War,* André Deutsch, 1973.

Bell, P., *Chamberlain, Germany and Japan 1933–1934*, Macmillan, 1996.

Bessell, R., *Nazism and War*, Weidenfeld and Nicolson, 2004.

Betts, R.F., *France and Decolonization, 1900–1960*, Macmillan, 1991.

Bialer, U., *The Shadow of the Bomber; the Fear of Air Attack and British Politics 1932–1939*, Royal Historical Society, 1980.

Bloch, M., *Ribbentrop*, Bantam Press, 1992.

Bond, B., *British Military Policy between the Wars*, Oxford University Press, 1980.

Boyce, R. (ed.), *Paths to War: Essays on the Origins of the Second World War*, Macmillan, 1989.

Boyce, R. and Maiolo, J.A. (eds), *The Origins of World War Two: The Debate Continues*, Palgrave, 2003.

Bullock, A., *Hitler and Stalin: Parallel Lives*, Harper Collins, 1991.

Butow, R.J., *Tojo and the Coming of War*, Princeton University Press, 1961.

Carley, M.J., *1939: The Alliance that never was and the coming of World War II*, Ivan R. Dee, Chicago, 1999.

Carr, W., *Arms, Autarky and Aggression*, Arnold, 1972.

Carroll, B.A., *Design for Total War: Arms and Economics in the Third Reich*, Mouton, The Hague, 1968.

Catterall, P. and Morris, C.J. (eds), *Britain and the Threat to Stability in Europe 1918–1945*, Leicester University Press, 1993.

Charmley, J., *Chamberlain and the Lost Peace*, Hodder, 1989.

Chickering, R., Förster, S. and Greiner, B. (eds), *A World at Total War: Global Conflict and the Politics of Destruction, 1937–1945*, Cambridge University Press, 2005.

Cienciala, A., *Poland and the Western Powers, 1938–9*, Routledge, 1968.

Clavin, P., *The Failure of Economic Diplomacy: Britain, Germany, France and the United States 1931–1936*, Macmillan, 1996.

Clavin, P., *The Great Depression in Europe, 1929–1939*, Palgrave, 2000.

Crowley, J.B., *Japan's Quest for Autonomy; National Security and Foreign Policy 1930–1938*, Princeton University Press, 1966.

Deist, W., *The Wehrmacht and German Rearmament*, Macmillan, 1981.

Deist, W., Messerschmidt, M., Volkmann, H-E. and Wette, W., *Germany and the Second World War: Volume I, the Build-Up of German Aggression*, Oxford University Press, 1990.

Delzell, C. (ed.), *Mediterranean Fascism 1919–1945*, Macmillan, 1971.

Dilks, D. (ed.), *Retreat from Power. Studies in Britain's Foreign Policy in the Twentieth Century*, 2 vols, Macmillan, 1981.

Divine, R.A., *The Reluctant Belligerent. American Entry into World War II*, John Wiley, New York, 1965.

Drummond, I.M., *Imperial Economic Policy 1917–1939*, George Allen and Unwin, 1974.

Dull, P.S., *A Battle History of the Imperial Japanese Navy 1941–1945*, Cambridge University Press, 1978.

Dutton, D., *Neville Chamberlain*, Edward Arnold, 2001.

Feiling, K., *The Life of Neville Chamberlain*, Macmillan, 1946.

Finney, P. (ed.), *The Origins of the Second World War*, Arnold, 1997.

Fox, J.P., *Germany and the Far Eastern Crisis 1931–1938*, Oxford University Press, 1982.

Frankenstein, R., *Le prix du réarmement français, 1935–1939*, Sorbonne, Paris, 1982.

French, D., *Raising Churchill's Army: The British Army and the War against Germany 1919–1945*, Oxford University Press, 2000.

Friedländer, S., *Prelude to Downfall: Hitler and the United States 1939–1941*, Chatto and Windus, 1967.

Gibbs, N., *Grand Strategy: Volume I, Rearmament Policy*, HMSO, 1976.

Glantz, D., *Stumbling Colossus: The Red Army on the Eve of World War*, University of Kansas Press, Lawrence, Kansas, 1998.

Gorodetsky, G., *Grand Delusion: Stalin and the German Invasion of Russia*, Yale University Press, New Haven, 1999.

Haggie, P., *Britannia at Bay: the Defence of the British Empire against Japan 1931–1941*, Oxford University Press, 1981.

Haight, J.M., *American Aid to France 1938–1940*, Atheneum, New York, 1981.

Haslam, J., *The Soviet Union and the Struggle for Collective Security 1933–1939*, Macmillan, 1984.

Heinemann, J.L., *Hitler's First Foreign Minister*, Berkeley University Press, 1979.

Heinrichs, W., *Threshold of War: Franklin D. Roosevelt & American Entry into World War II*, Oxford University Press, 1988.

Herzstein, R.E., *When Nazi Dreams Come True: The Third Reich's Internal Struggle over the Future of Europe*, Sphere Books, 1982.

Hildebrand, K., *The Foreign Policy of the Third Reich*, Batsford, 1973.

Hillgruber, A., *Germany and Two World Wars*, Harvard University Press, 1981.

Hinsley, F.H., *Power and the Pursuit of Peace*, Cambridge University Press, 1969.

Homze, E., *Arming the Luftwaffe*, University of Nebraska Press, 1976.

Howard, M., *The Continental Commitment*, Temple Smith, 1972.

Imlay, T., *Facing the Second World War: Strategy, Politics, and Economics in Britain and France, 1938–1940*, Oxford University Press, 2003.

Jackson, P., *France and the Nazi Menace: Intelligence and Policy Making 1933–1939*, Oxford University Press, 2000.

Jones, F.C., *Japan's New Order in East Asia*, Oxford University Press, 1954.

Kaiser, D., *Economic Diplomacy and the Origins of the Second World War*, Princeton University Press, 1980.

Kemp, T., *The French Economy 1913–1939: the History of a Decline*, Longman, 1972.

Kennedy, P., *The Rise and Fall of the Great Powers*, Unwin Hyman, 1988.

Kershaw, I., *Fateful Choices: Ten Decisions that Changed the World*, Penguin/Allen Lane, 2007.

Kindleberger, C.I., *The World in Depression 1929–1939*, Allen Lane, 1973.

King, A., *Memorials of the Great War in Britain: The Symbolism and Politics of Remembrance*, Oxford University Press, 1998.

Kley, S., *Hitler, Ribbentrop und die Entfesselung des Zweiten Weltkrieges*, Schöningh, Paderborn, 1996.

Knox, M., *Mussolini Unleashed, 1939–1941*, Cambridge University Press, 1983.

Lacaze, Y., *France and Munich: a Study in Decision Making in International Affairs*, Columbia University Press, New York, 1995.

Langhorne, R., *The Collapse of the Concert of Europe: International Politics 1890–1914*, Macmillan, 1981.

Leach, B., *German Strategy against Russia 1939–1941*, Oxford University Press, 1973.

Lee, B.A., *Britain and the Sino-Japanese War 1937–1939*, Stanford University Press, 1973.

Louis, W.R., *British Strategy in the Far East 1919–1939*, Oxford University Press, 1971.

Lowe, P., *Great Britain and the Origins of the Pacific War*, Oxford University Press, 1977.

Lukes, I. and Goldstein, E. (eds), *The Munich Crisis, 1938: Prelude to World War II*, Frank Cass, 1999.

Macdonald, C., *The United States, Britain and Appeasement 1936–1939*, Macmillan, 1981.

Mack Smith, D., *Mussolini's Roman Empire*, Longman, 1976.

Macmillan, M., *Peacemakers: The Paris Conference of 1919 and its Attempt to End War*, John Murray, 2001.

Maiolo, J.A., *The Royal Navy and Nazi Germany, 1933–39*, Palgrave, 1998.

Mallett, R., *The Italian Navy and Fascist Expansionism 1935–1940*, Frank Cass, 1998.

Marks, S., *The Illusion of Peace: International Relations in Europe 1918–1933*, Macmillan, 1979.

Marks, S., *The Ebbing of European Ascendancy: An International History of the World 1914–1945*, Hodder Arnold, 2002.

Martel, G. (ed.), *The Origins of the Second World War Reconsidered: A.J.P. Taylor and the Historians*, Routledge, 1999.

May, E.R. (ed.), *Knowing One's Enemies: Intelligence Assessments before the Two World Wars*, Princeton University Press, 1984.

May, E.R., *Strange Victory: Hitler's Conquest of France*, Hill and Wang, New York, 2000.

McCarthy, J., *The Ottoman Peoples and the End of Empire*, Hodder Arnold, 2001.

Milward, A.S., *The German Economy at War*, Athlone Press, 1965.

Mommsen, W. and Kettenacker, L. (eds), *The Fascist Challenge and the Policy of Appeasement*, George Allen and Unwin, 1983.

Murray, W., *The Change in the European Balance of Power 1938–1939*, Princeton University Press, 1984.

Néré, J., *The Foreign Policy of France from 1914–1945*, Routledge, 1975.

Nekrich, A., *Pariahs, Partners, Predators: German-Soviet Relations 1922–1941*, Columbia University Press, New York, 1997.

Newman, S., *March 1939: the British Guarantee to Poland*, Oxford University Press, 1976.

Newton, S., *Profits of Peace: the Political Economy of Anglo-German Appeasement*, Oxford University Press, 1996.

Nish, I., *Japanese Foreign Policy 1869–1942*, Routledge, 1977.

Northedge, F.S., *The Troubled Giant: Britain among the Great Powers 1916–1939*, London School of Economics, 1966.

Northedge, F.S., *The League of Nations: its Life and Times*, Leicester University Press, 1986.

Offner, A.A., *American Appeasement: United States Foreign Policy 1933–1938*, Harvard University Press, 1969.

Offner, A.A., *The Origins of the Second World War: American Foreign Policy and World Politics 1917–1941*, Praeger, New York, 1975.

Ovendale, R., *'Appeasement' and the English-Speaking World 1937–1939*, University of Wales Press, Cardiff, 1975.

Overy, R.J., *The Air War 1939–1945*, 3rd edn, Potomac Books, 2006.

Overy, R.J., *Goering: the 'Iron Man'*, Routledge, 1984.

Overy, R.J., *The Inter-War Crisis 1919–1939*, 2nd edn, Longman, 2007.

Overy, R.J., *War and Economy in the Third Reich*, Oxford University Press, 1994b.

Overy, R.J. with Wheatcroft, A., *The Road to War*, 2nd edn, Macmillan, 1998.

Overy, R.J., *The Dictators: Hitler's Germany and Stalin's Russia*, Penguin/Allen Lane, 2004.

Parker, R.A.C., *Chamberlain and Appeasement: British Policy and the Coming of the Second World War*, Macmillan, 1993.

Parker, R.A.C., *Churchill and Appeasement: Could Churchill have Prevented the Second World War?*, Macmillan Press, 2000.

Peden, G.C., *British Rearmament and the Treasury 1932–1939*, Scottish Academic Press, Edinburgh, 1979.

Pons, S., *Stalin and the Inevitable War, 1936–1941*, Palgrave, 2002.

Porch, D., *The French Secret Service: from the Dreyfus Affair to the Gulf War*, Macmillan, 1993.

Porter, B., *The Lion's Share: a Short History of British Imperialism 1850–1995*, 3rd edn, Longman, 1996.

Pratt, L.R., *East of Malta, West of Suez: Britain's Mediterranean Crisis 1936–1939*, Cambridge University Press, 1975.

Prazmowska, A., *Britain, Poland and the Eastern Front, 1939*, Cambridge University Press, 1987.

Prazmowska, A., *Eastern Europe and the Origins of the Second World War*, Macmillan Press, 2000.

Preston, A., *General Staffs and Diplomacy before the Second World War*, Croom Helm, 1978.

Ragsdale, H., *The Soviets, the Munich Crisis, and the Coming of World War II*, Cambridge University Press, 2004.

Reynolds, D., *The Creation of the Anglo-American Alliance 1937–1941*, Europa, 1981.

Reynolds, D., *Britannia Overruled: British Policy and World Power in the Twentieth Century*, Longman, 1991.

Roberts, G., *The Soviet Union and the Origins of the Second World War: Russo-German Relations and the Road to War 1933–1941*, Macmillan, 1995.

Roberts, G., *Stalin's Wars*, Yale University Press, 2006.

Robertson, E.M., *Hitler's Pre-War Policy and Military Plans*, Longman, 1963.

Robertson, E.M., *Mussolini as Empire-Builder,* Macmillan, 1977.

Robertson, E.M. (ed.), *The Origins of the Second World War*, Macmillan, 1971.

Rock, W., *Chamberlain and Roosevelt: British Foreign Policy and the United States, 1939–1940*, Ohio State University Press, 1988.

Rossino, A.B., *Hitler Strikes Poland: Blitzkrieg, Ideology and Atrocity*, University Press of Kansas, Lawrence, Kansas, 2003.

Samuelson, L., *Plans for Stalin's War Machine: Tukhachevskii and Military-Economic Planning, 1925–1941*, Macmillan, 2000.

Schmidt, G., *England in der Krise: Grundzüge und Grundlagen der Britischen Appeasement-Politik*, Westdeutscher Verlag, Opladen, 1981.

Schmitz, D.F. and Challener, R. D. (eds), *Appeasement in Europe: a Reassessment of US Policies*, Greenwood Press, New York, 1990.

Shay, R., *British Rearmament in the Thirties*, Princeton University Press, 1977.

Steiner, Z., *The Lights that Failed: European International History 1919–1933*, Oxford University Press, 2005.

Sun, Y., *China and the Origins of the Pacific War 1931–1941*, St Martin's Press, New York, 1993.

Taylor, A.J.P., *The Origins of the Second World War*, Hamish Hamilton, 1961.

Teichova, A., *An Economic Background to Munich*, Cambridge University Press, 1974.

Thorne, C., *The Approach of War 1938–1939*, Macmillan, 1967.

Tooze, A., *The Wages of Destruction: The Making and Breaking of the Nazi Economy*, Penguin/Allen Lane, 2006.

Ulam, A., *Expansion and Coexistence: a History of Soviet Foreign Policy 1917–1967*, Secker and Warburg, 1968.

Vyšný, P., *The Runciman Mission to Czechoslovakia 1938*, Palgrave, 2003.

Wark, W.K., *The Ultimate Enemy: British Intelligence and Nazi Germany 1933–1939*, Oxford University Press, 1986.

Watt, D.C., *How War Came: the Immediate Origins of the Second World War 1938–1939*, Heinemann, 1989.

Wegner, B. (ed.), *From Peace to War: Germany, Soviet Russia, and the World 1939–1941*, Berghahn Books, Oxford, 1997.

Weinberg, G., *The Foreign Policy of Hitler's Germany 1933–1936*, University of Chicago Press, 1970.

Weinberg, G., *Hitler's Foreign Policy 1937–1939*, University of Chicago Press, 1980.

Weinberg, G., *World in the Balance*, New England University Press, 1981.

Weinberg, G., *Visions of Victory: The Hopes of Eight World War II Leaders*, Cambridge University Press, 2005.

Wendt, B.-J., *'Economic Appeasement': Handel und Finanz in der Britischen Deutschlandpolitik 1933–1939*, Bertelsmann Universitätsverlag, 1971.

Winter, J. and Baggett, B., *The Great War and the Shaping of the Twentieth Century*, BBC Books, 1996.

Werth, A., *France and Munich*, Hamish Hamilton, 1939.

Young, R.J., *In Command of France: French Foreign Policy and Military Planning 1933–1940*, Harvard University Press, 1978a.

Young, R.J., *France and the Origins of the Second World War*, Macmillan, 1996.

Secondary sources: articles

Barnhart, M., 'Japan's economic security and the origins of the Pacific war', *Journal of Strategic Studies*, 4, 1981.

Blaazer, D., 'Finance and the end of appeasement: The bank of England, the national government and Czech gold', *Journal of Contemporary History*, 40, 2005.

Buffotot, P., 'The French High Command and the Franco-Soviet Alliance 1933–1939', *Journal of Strategic Studies*, 5, 1982.

Carley, M., 'Soviet foreign policy and the West, 1936–1941', *Europe-Asia Studies*, 56, 2004.

Catalano, F., 'Les ambitions Mussoliniennes et la réalité économique de l'Italie', *Revue d'Histoire de la Deuxième Guerre Mondiale*, 17, 1967.

Coghlan, F., 'Armaments, economic policy and appeasement: background to British foreigh policy 1931–7', *History*, 57, 1972.

Crozier, A., 'Imperial decline and the colonial question in Anglo-German relations 1919–1939', *European Studies Review*, 11, 1981.

Frank, W.C., 'The Spanish Civil War and the coming of the Second World War', *International History Review*, 9, 1987.

Haslam, J., 'The Soviet Union and the Czech crisis', *Journal of Contemporary History*, 14, 1979.

Hauner, M., 'Did Hitler want a world dominion?', *Journal of Contemporary History*, 13, 1978.

Herman, J., 'Soviet peace efforts on the eve of World War Two', *Journal of Contemporary History*, 15, 1980.

Hillgruber, A., 'England's place in Hitler's plan for world dominion', *Journal of Contemporary History*, 9, 1974.

Imlay, T. and Horn, M., 'Money in wartime: France's financial preparation for the two world wars', *International History Review*, 27, 2005.

Jackson, P., 'France and the guarantee to Romania, April 1939', *Intelligence and National Security*, 10, 1995.

Johnson, G., 'British policy towards Europe, 1919–1939', *The Historical Journal*, 46, 2003.

Kimball, W. F., 'Beggar my neighbour: America and the British interim finance crisis 1940–1941', *Journal of Economic History*, 29, 1969.

Lukes, I. 'Stalin and Beneš in the final days of September 1938', *Slavic Review*, 52, 1993.

Macdonald, C.A., 'Economic appeasement and the German "Moderates" 1937–1939', *Past & Present*, no. 56, 1972.

Manne, R., 'The British decision for alliance with Russia, May 1939', *Journal of Contemporary History*, 9, 1974.

Manne, R., 'Some British light on the Nazi-Soviet Pact', *European Studies Review*, 11, 1981.

Mason, T.W., 'Some origins of the Second World War', *Past & Present*, no. 29, 1964.

Mason, T.W., 'Labour in the Third Reich', *Past & Present*, no. 33, 1966.

Mawdsley, E., 'Crossing the Rubicon: Soviet plans for offensive war 1940–1941', *International History Review*, 26, 2004.

McKercher, B., '"Our most dangerous enemy": Britain pre-eminent in the 1930s', *International History Review*, 13, 1991.

Michaelis, M., 'World power status or world dominion?', *Historical Journal*, 15, 1972.

Offner, A.A., 'Appeasement revisited. The US, Great Britain, and Germany 1933–1940', *Journal of American History*, 64, 1977.

Overy, R.J., 'The German Motorisierung and rearmament', *Economic History Review*, 2nd Ser., 32, 1979.

Overy, R.J., 'Germany, "Domestic Crisis" and war in 1939', *Past & Present*, no. 116, 1987.

Overy, R.J., 'Mobilization for total war in Germany 1939–1941', *English Historical Review*, 103, 1988.

Overy, R.J., 'Strategic intelligence and the outbreak of the Second World War', *War in History*, 5, 1998.

Overy, R.J., Kaiser, D. and Mason, T., 'Debate: Germany, "Domestic Crisis" and war in 1939', *Past & Present*, no. 122, 1989.

Parker, R.A.C., 'British rearmament 1936–1939: Treasury, trade unions and skilled labour', *English Historical Review*, 96, 1981.

Parker, R.A.C., 'The pound sterling, the American treasury, and British preparations for war 1938–1939', *English Historical Review*, 98, 1983.

Peden, G.C., 'A matter of timing: the economic background to British foreign policy 1938–1939', *History*, 69, 1984.

Reynolds, D., '1940: fulcrum of the twentieth century', *International Affairs*, 66, 1990.

Richardson, C.O., 'French plans for allied attacks on the Caucasus Oilfelds, Jan–Apr. 1940', *French Historical Studies*, 8, 1973.

Roberts, G., 'The fall of Litvinov: a revisionist view', *Journal of Contemporary History*, 27, 1992.

Schatz, A.W., 'The Anglo-American Trade Agreement and Cordell Hull's search for peace 1936–1938', *Journal of American History*, 57, 1970–1.

Simpson, A.E., 'The struggle for control of the German economy 1936/7', *Journal of Modern History*, 21, 1959.

Stafford, P., 'The French government and the Danzig crisis: the Italian dimension', *International History Review*, 6, 1984.

Steiner, Z., 'The Soviet Commissariat of Foreign Affairs and the Czechoslovakian crisis in 1938: new material from the Soviet archives', *The Historical Journal*, 42, 1999.

Tamchina, R., 'In search of common causes. The Imperial Conference of 1937', *Journal of Imperial and Commonwealth History*, 1, 1972.

Thomas, M., 'Economic conditions and the limits to mobilization in the French Empire, 1936–1939', *The Historical Journal*, 48, 2005.

Thomson, D., 'The era of violence', *New Cambridge Modern History*, vol. 12, Cambridge University Press, 1960.

Young, R.J., 'The strategic dream: French air doctrine in the inter-war period 1919–39', *Journal of Contemporary History*, 9, 1974.

Young, R.J., 'La guerre de longue durée: some reflections on French strategy and diplomacy in the 1930s' in Preston, A. (ed.), *General Staffs and Diplomacy before the Second World War*, Croom Helm, 1978.

Index

9781405874342

SEMINAR STUDIES
IN HISTORY

9780582771895

9781405874366

9781405874359

9780582299085

9781405874311

9781405874304

9781405874328

9781405840583

9781405874335

9781405824699

9781405812535

Other books available in this series

Full Title	Author	ISBN
The First World War 2nd Edition	Stuart Robson	978-1-4058-2471-2
The Russian Revolution 2nd Edition	A. Wood	978-0-582-35559-0
Lenin's Revolution:Russia, 1917-1921	David Marples	978-0-582-31917-2
Fascism and the Right in Europe 1919-1945	Martin Blinkhorn	978-0-582-07021-9
Anti-Semitism before the Holocaust	Albert S. Lindemann	978-0-582-36964-1
The Holocaust: The Third Reich and the Jews	David Engel	978-0-582-32720-7
The Third Reich 3rd Edition	D.G. Williamson	978-0-582-36883-5
The Second World War in Europe	S. P. Mackenzie	978-1-4058-4699-8
Hitler and the Rise of the Nazi Party	Frank McDonough	978-1-582-50606-8
Japan in Transformation, 1952-2000	Jeffrey Kingston	978-0-582-41875-2
China since 1949	Linda Benson	978-0-582-35722-8
Eastern Europe 1945-1969: From Stalinism to Stagnation	Ben Fowkes	978-0-582-32693-4
The Khrushchev Era 1953-1964	Martin McCauley	978-0-582-27776-2
The Origins of the Vietnam War	Fredrik Logevall	978-0-582-31918-9
The Collapse of the Soviet Union, 1985-1991	David Marples	978-0-582-50599-1
The United Nations since 1945: Peacekeeping and the Cold War	Norrie MacQueen	978-0-582-35673-3
South Africa: The Rise and Fall of Apartheid	Nancy Clark and William H Worgew	978-0-582-41437-2
Race and Empire	Jane Samson	978-0-582-41837-0